Carol Klein
Making a Garden

Successful Gardening by Nature's Rules

Photography by Jonathan Buckley

MITCHELL BEAZLEY

contents

woodland

seaside

exposed

*This book is dedicated
to all those who inspire us all
through their gardens,
by listening to Mother Earth
and heeding her words.*

hedgerow

150

wetland

188

meadow

236

I love my garden. Next to gardening itself, I relish talking about gardening and writing about it. This is a book I have been longing to do. I hope it expresses what I feel about gardening and what for me is the foundation on which it is based. Nature is the best of teachers and if we observe how she operates and base our own efforts on what we can learn from her, we stand a good chance of creating beautiful gardens.

Looking & Learning

OUR GARDENS MAY BE cultivated places but each of them is comparable to a wild habitat. By looking at the wild environments that most closely resemble our own plots we can obtain much of the basic information we need to get gardening.

With its attempt to break down and refine these natural environments in greater detail, this book could have had a hundred chapters – or more. However, I have kept it to six broad categories: woodland, seaside, exposed, hedgerow, wetland, and meadow. Many of our gardens contain elements of several of these within their boundaries. The chapter about hedgerows, for example, has relevance for just about all our gardens.

At Glebe Cottage, in north Devon, UK, one side of my garden is open and sunny, there are terraced beds and borders and, for me, this area equates to a meadow with colonies of herbaceous plants and grasses happily mixing and mingling, cheek by jowl. On the east side of the track, starting only a few metres away, conditions are different; from the time the tall beeches (*Fagus*) to the south of this area come into glorious leaf, the whole place is thrown into shade. Though it would be pompous to call this woodland, if I look to the woods when thinking of what conditions pertain here and which plants to grow, there are clear signposts on how to proceed.

Opposite – My garden should be a happy place where the plants I have put in and those that have invited themselves have just what they need not only to survive but also to thrive. In a shady spot under a weeping pear (Pyrus), columbines (Aquilegia) and Welsh poppies (Meconopsis cambrica) join in the fun, and I am lucky enough to sit among them.

Most woodlanders under deciduous trees are spring plants –
Cinderellas (see p.14). The first snowdrops (*Galanthus*), lily of the
valley (*Convallaria*), and bluebells (*Hyacinthoides*) all rush to shoot
through the warming ground, flower, set seed, then die back, resting
until the next year's warm spring sun spurs them into growth.

There are boggy areas in my garden, too, and a little pond, and
here we take our cue from wetlands – the lakes, bogs, rivers, and
streams that criss-cross the countryside.

Mother Nature

The way we garden is governed by natural laws. If we plant our bulbs
upside down, they will struggle to come up. If we bury fine seeds
deep in heavy clay in the middle of a prolonged cold spell, they are
unlikely to germinate. Thus common sense is the most important
rule of gardening. When we are not sure about something, if we look
at what Nature does – how she behaves and what she decrees – and
we try to emulate her, we are well on the way to success.

These natural processes take place not in the abstract but very
much on the ground. Our own gardens are the places where we apply
the lessons we learn. For the great majority of gardeners, the plants
are of the greatest importance. Although we may inherit a garden
with trees, shrubs, perennials, and bulbs, sometimes we do have to
start from scratch.

Whatever the gardening situation, what matters most is to
understand what our gardens have, where they are and how various
factors – soil, aspect, climate and place – influence them.

If we can grasp the essence of our gardens, we can make the right
choices about how to treat them and which plants to grow. This book
does not pretend to offer formulae, rules to follow, boxes to tick, or
infallible solutions. Every garden is different and every gardener
too – that is the fun of it. Gardening is always a question of trial and
error, of experiment, and of adventure.

The climate and conditions that pertain in the British Isles are
infinitely varied. Although we can identify what conditions our
plots are subject to, the problems we may face, or the benefits we
may enjoy, this is sometimes considered as an afterthought, whereas
really it should be our first stop.

Some 35 years ago, when Neil and I moved to Glebe Cottage,
I had very little experience of gardening. I was so thrilled to have
a garden, a plot of my own, where I could finally grow the plants of
my dreams – all those wonderful plants whose pictures I had looked

Above left and centre – At home we note plants that are happy and grow more of them, often from seed collected in the garden. Here, more Scabiosa columbaria subsp. ochroleuca *and* Stipa tenuissima *are heading for a sunny, well-drained spot at the end of a raised bed – a very exposed spot.* Eryngium bourgatii (above centre) *will join them.*

Above right – One of the joys of walking in your locality is to gather inspiration for your own garden. It is not so much taking careful notes of what is growing as of getting a feel for what will thrive in similar conditions back home. Hedgerows are relevant not just to the countryside but to all our gardens too.

at for years and, among them, a few that I had actually met face to face on occasional garden visits or while looking over people's walls or through their fences. The world was my horticultural oyster.

Since then there have been a few failures and occasional disasters. We did not have much money and since most of our plants were home-propagated – from seeds and cuttings – there was not any huge financial loss. Lessons were gradually learned. Nowadays, if I am thinking about buying a plant, I imagine taking it home, putting it in the middle of the track that runs through our garden, and thinking of where it would take itself if it had feet. If it were not able to find anywhere it would feel at home, then I must forget it.

Ever since Nicola Ferguson coined the phrase "right plant, right place" when she wrote her wonderful book of the same name, prompted by the problems she faced – and solved – in her own shady Edinburgh garden, we gardeners have focused on how to go about selecting our plants. By first-hand observation and consulting Nature at every possible opportunity, we can make not just the right choice of plants, but also endeavour to use our plants in ways that fit the place in which they are to grow.

This gardening book is different from most. It will not offer foolproof solutions or quick-fix formulae to solve all your horticultural woes, but I hope that, as you read, it will prompt you to think about where you garden, the similarities your plot has to wild habitats, and the sort of plants that will enjoy living there.

woodland

Everyone has a favourite sort of wild place. For my mum, it was a mountain top. She loved feeling the wind in her hair and the sun on her face. She was connected to the openness, in tune with the freedom of it. For me, it is the magic, the mystery of woodland to which I feel akin, the silence that is broken only when the twigs snap underneath your feet, the scent of moss, and the very earth itself. Sometimes you can smell deer and see where they have broken through the fallen branches and tangled honeysuckle that festoons them, to feast on the lichen or the tree bark.

Gardening in a Woodland-Style Habitat

Opposite – Gardening with woodlanders is very often done eye to eye, and the care (you give them/ they need) is often intimate and absorbing. The burnished foliage of these epimediums had given a brave show all winter long, when other plants were hiding underground. I should have sheared them back earlier, but sometimes it is worth enjoying them for as long as possible, even when that means painstaking trimming when new leaves and flowers are on their way.

WOODS ARE SECRET PLACES where anything is imaginable. Every wood has its own presence. Few of us are lucky enough to have our own wood or even to be close to one, but the moment we have shade in our garden the whole possibility of creating that feeling becomes a reality. I love trees but it is the plants that grow underneath them, the woodlanders, that really seduce me. They may be little flowers, but they have a giant charisma.

Shade is often seen as a major problem. It may be cast by man-made objects – buildings, walls, or fences – or by plants – hedges, trees, and shrubs. In urban gardens, shade is often a combination of both. At ground level this may result in large shadowy areas with dry, impoverished soil, reason enough for most of us to wring our hands and gnash our teeth. But before anyone throws in the horticultural t(r)owel, it is worth looking at how Mother Nature deals with similar circumstances and see what plants we can grow in our own gardens wherever shadows are cast.

In dense conifer forest, the woodland floor can offer other plants – perennials, annuals, and bulbs – very little hospitality. But deciduous woodland is a totally different proposition. During the winter in most temperate regions, it is too cold for perennial plants to flourish. There are exceptions, of course: evergreen perennials.

13

Above – Stems of Cornus alba *'Sibirica' glow in the winter light, while all around them, relishing the damp ground, snowdrops insinuate themselves among the cornus roots, carpeting the whole thicket with their optimistic flowers. This is a combination that could be used on a small scale in a damp, shady corner of any garden.*

*Opposite – Double snowdrops (*Galanthus nivalis *f.* pleniflorus *'Flore Pleno') wander through the woods. Their inexorable progress and their promise of spring gladden hearts and introduce optimism for the year ahead. They are the easiest of bulbs to grow, trouble-free and rewarding. Divide them every couple of years, and their increase will be exponential.*

Of these, hellebores are probably the prime example, from forms of *Helleborus × hybridus* to UK-native stinking hellebores (*H. foetidus*) and *H. viridis*. Pulmonarias make a brave show too, and there are bulbs – the snowdrop is the most obvious – that brave the elements.

But, come the first few warm days, the woodland floor is the place to be! The branches may be bare overhead – that is part of the picture – but, below, the bare ground is transformed, the dull, lank leaf litter is suddenly spangled with myriad tiny flowers. These "Cinderella plants" have to rush to achieve everything before the canopy fills in overhead, depriving them of light and moisture. They must push up through the cold earth, open their flowers, attract pollinators, set seed, disperse it, and then disappear before the clock strikes 12.

There are other plants that capitalize on extra light at the other end of the summer. When the leaf canopy thins out in the autumn and more light becomes available, Japanese anemones, kirengeshoma, and the lovely *Cyclamen hederifolium* come into their own.

Far from presenting a problem, shade therefore allows us to grow some of the most enchanting plants on the planet.

Right – All the winter-flowering viburnums have a sweet scent, none more fragrant than forms of Viburnum carlesii. *In this cultivar, V. c. 'Aurora', the buds are deep pink, almost crimson, and the flowers are flushed with pink. Most start to flower as young shrubs and produce their heavenly scented blooms reliably every early and mid-spring after that.*

Far right – At Glebe Cottage, we do not go in much for rhododendrons, yet R. 'Lady Alice Fitzwilliam' has become a cherished plant. When its trusses of flowers of soft pink touched with amber are full out in mid- and late spring, a daily trip to drink in their delicious nutmeg fragrance is a must.

Opposite – On a bleak mid-winter day, when its spreading branches are lit with pale yellow tassels, Hamamelis × intermedia 'Pallida' *makes an invaluable antidote and sounds an optimistic note for the year ahead. To glimpse the earth between its spreading growth, bare until a few weeks before but now embellished with snowdrops and winter aconites, reinforces the message.*

Scent secrets in winter

Colour, form, and texture are all facets of gardening that can be described in words or portrayed in Jonathan's wonderful pictures. Scent is the factor that is so omnipresent but so intangible and is especially important in winter. There are scented shrubs aplenty that thrive in a shady setting – *Viburnum × bodnantense* and *V. farreri*, mahonias, and winter-flowering honeysuckles. All have perfume that carries in the air, a timely reminder that, far from being a dead place, the winter garden is alive and revving up for spring.

Despite the cold weather, in the middle of our woodland garden *Hamamelis × intermedia* 'Pallida' has opened its pale, spidery flowers and its gentle scent pervades the whole area. The lemon-yellow flowers show up particularly well against a dark backdrop, but if you want a warmer colour to counteract the chill in the air, try *H. × i.* 'Jelena', with its coppery orange flowers, or *H. × i.* 'Feuerzauber', a buxom cultivar with an upright habit that produces big flowers the colour of a blood orange.

There are other scented flowers whose proper season is now. Algerian iris (*Iris unguicularis*) has large, violet flowers with a beautifully sweet scent; this is especially rich when cut and brought into a warm room.

Many bulbs have scented flowers too. While most snowdrops produce a delicate scent, *Galanthus* 'S. Arnott' is exceptional. Its large, rounded, white bells give off a glorious, honeyed perfume.

Opposite – Iris *'Katharine Hodgkin'* is unique, probably a cross between I. histrioides *and* I. winogradowii. *Just a few centimetres tall, it has more flower-power than many a tall iris. And what flowers it has too – soft silvery blue with an intricate tracery of darker lines and egg-yolk-yellow centres; everybody falls in love with it.*

Right – Narcissus *'W.P. Milner' is a delightful lemon-yellow that naturalizes well and associates seamlessly with so many plants, as shown here planted with* Lysimachia ciliata *'Firecracker'.*

Below – In the shady part of my garden, there are countless Narcissus *'Thalia', a white triandrus narcissus. When it finishes flowering, its faded flowers are removed promptly so that no energy is wasted setting seed. Foliage is discarded only when it has started to yellow and slump and the bulb has reabsorbed all its goodness.*

Overleaf – Allium triquetrum *carpets the nut garden at Sissinghurst, Kent, UK. It is in complete control.*

Spring bulbs

Some woodland bulbs are native to the UK – ransoms (wild garlic), daffodils, bluebells, and snowdrops, the last perhaps not originally indigenous but accepted as part of the UK floral heritage. No doubt, ransoms, daffodils, and bluebells predate humans by thousands, perhaps millions, of years. They (and snowdrops too) have evolved not only to cope with shade but to thrive in it, and the woodland floor is their element. Once these bulbs have flowered and set seed, their mission for the year is accomplished; their foliage fizzles, swelling the bulb as it sinks into its summer sleep until once again, as next spring calls, it rises phoenix-like to beautify our shady corners.

Which plant best personifies spring? For optimists, it is the snowdrop, for realists, the primrose, but for most, it must be the daffodil. Nothing says spring so categorically. *Narcissus pseudonarcissus* is small (23cm/9in), strong, and stocky. The flowers of this wild daffodil emerge from a papery spathe, gently turning themselves downwards to protect pollen and to shelter obliging insects inside their deep yellow trumpets. The outer perianth is a pale soft yellow. These are Wordsworth's host, the Lent lily.

In a shady garden setting, forms of this and other small narcissi are in keeping. So too are the legion of little, blue bulbs that make themselves at home in the same circumstances. Most, like woodlanders native to the UK, are opportunists, seeding themselves around and colonizing happily. There are scillas, chionodoxa, and muscari, as well as the beautiful *Iris* 'Katharine Hodgkin'.

Opposite – In Lilium *'Mrs R.O. Backhouse' the combination of pink-flushed buds, opening to flowers of softest apricot splodged with chocolate and finished with marmalade orange anthers, is almost too much to take in. This is one of the most desirable lilies ever and is the result of a cross between a martagon lily and* Lilium hansonii *made almost a hundred years ago.*

Below – Martagon lilies have a wide distribution in the wild, but all frequent woodland margins. Their informality is made-to-measure for the spaces between shrubs and in the dappled shade cast by trees with light canopies such as birch and cherry. They may take a couple of years to settle in but will seed themselves around if they are happy.

Summer bulbs

One of the perceived problems with shady gardens is that they are most celebrated in the early part of the year . Spring-flowering, shade-loving bulbs are easy to locate, but what of later? Which bulbs will adore living in cool, shady places and yet come into their own after the canopy has filled in overhead or, in a city garden, cope with permanent shade yet still ornament the shadows in summer?

Fortunately, many lilies are woodlanders, and in their native habitats often establish colonies. Though martagon lilies are the classic shade-loving lily, there are species from eastern Asia and America that also feel perfectly at home in dappled shade.

We once had a fine clump of leopard lilies (*Lilium pardalinum*), whose reflexed petals were gorgeously spotted and from which protruded dangling anthers were almost expelled, pushed forward by the flowers. They increased gradually year by year until I drained the area where they were growing so happily. They faltered and eventually gave up the ghost. Only later did I discover that I had killed them – they are one of the few lilies that must have moist soil.

Fantastic ferns

In our part of Devon, the high banks positively drip with polypody, one of the most enduring and most useful of evergreen ferns. It spreads slowly, establishing large colonies. Even when this fern is butchered by mechanical hedge trimmers, its fronds quickly resprout. One garden variety, *Polypodium vulgare* 'Cornubiense', has finely cut fronds. Should the typical, plainer fronds reassert themselves, they should be removed promptly.

Polypody is often accompanied by the upright shuttlecocks of hart's tongue fern (*Asplenium scolopendrium*). Although it is not much taller than polypody, hart's tongue fern creates a much more architectural effect. There are several variations on the theme, including *A. s.* Crispum Group, whose undulating edges give a highly prized, frilly look. It contrasts well with low, clumping plants and the lacy filigree of many other ferns.

Soft shield fern (*Polystichum setiferum*) is one of my all-time favourites, and *P. s.* 'Plumosomultilobum Densum' creates a frothy effect. The central midrib of each frond is covered with shaggy, brown scales, and the fronds themselves are a lovely soft green.

When *Dryopteris erythrosora* unfurls its new fronds, they are decidedly orange but mature to a rich green. They are beautifully arched – just one plant set against a tree stump makes a fine picture. Broad buckler fern (*D. dilatata*) is just as graceful but deciduous.

Opposite – The handsome Himalayan fern Dryopteris wallichiana, *with its near-black midribs, forms the centrepiece alongside a mossy stump in a corner of our springtime shady garden. All the plants here are in full flow, including* Epimedium × versicolor *'Neosulphureum' with its new flowers and foliage. In the background a contingent of* Trillium chloropetalum *waits in the wings.*

Below left – Fern crosiers beginning to unfurl personify the excitement of spring energy.

Below right – As I cut back old fronds in the garden, I sniff the air. There is a scent attached to ferns – an indescribable odour of earth and all that is fundamental about the soil and what grows in it – that manages to combine the smell of decay and that of life.

Right – If you have room for only one tree trunk in your garden, then perhaps it should be Prunus serrula, *with its outstanding bark. Its high polish and rich chestnut colour make it a focal point wherever it is, especially in mid-winter. The froth of cow parsley, here the bronze-leaved version* Anthriscus sylvestris *'Ravenswing', makes the perfect foil for the strong, shiny stems of the cherry.*

Opposite above left – Frost emphasizes the pattern of the growing leaves of heuchera and the random ones of beech, fallen from the tree overhead.

*Opposite above centre – Strawberry tree (*Arbutus unedo*) and its cross* A. × andrachnoides *have rich, chestnut-coloured bark, which peels away. An ability to withstand coastal gales makes them perfect maritime trees.*

*Opposite above right – I have a weakness for katsura trees (*Cercidiphyllum*); there are seven in my little garden. This weeping form is the most graceful, with its curtain of pendulous branches.*

Opposite below left – Many acers, especially those hailing from the Orient, such as A. capillipes, *have handsome, striated bark. In addition, the new twigs of this species are pink and pretty.*

Opposite below centre – Nobody, young or old, can resist conkers. You just cannot help picking up and splitting the fruits asunder, discarding the spiky cases with their soft, felted interiors and turning the smooth, shiny, mahogany conker over and over in your hand.

Opposite below right – Interesting bark is a feature of most birches. Your fingertips may itch to peel the shaggy crust from some, such as this Betula nigra, *to reveal the pristine bark underneath.*

Trees & their brilliant bark

Even in the smallest garden there is room for a tree, but the smaller the garden, the more important its performance. We want a beautiful shape, a habit that fits in, the foliage must be outstanding, and the flowers and fruit too, and, in the case of deciduous trees, the silhouette and bark are paramount. Most trees that offer all this are naked for a full six months – half the year – and we need them to provide as much interest as possible during this time.

Many acers have exciting bark. Paper-bark maple (*A. griseum*) is prized for its shaggy trunk and branches, created by ever-peeling layers of tissue-thin bark. *Acer davidii*, also from China, has striking, stripy, green-and-white bark, hence its common name of snake-bark maple. Either could be accommodated in a medium-sized garden. As well as the winter interest created by their bark, both have glorious autumn colour, and the latter often boasts bunches of pendulous fruit, which turn red.

It is not just bark but coloured branches and twigs too that are at a premium during winter. *Acer palmatum* 'Sango-kaku', for example, makes a splendid specimen with its young twigs and branches of a bright, eye-catching pink.

Silver birch (*Betula pendula*) is also hard to beat. Its pale trunks are a striking feature in the winter landscape in the UK. For those who want something even more dramatic, *B. utilis* var. *jacquemontii* has such white bark that gardeners have been known to give it a regular scrub to maintain its sparkling stems.

Above – A shady corner can be given a theatrical twist by combining individual specimens, each in their own container, and using varying heights to display the thespian talents of the entire cast. With a backdrop of suitably dramatic foliage, the scene is set.

Opposite above and below – Evening-scented flowers release their perfume as dusk approaches. Most are pollinated by moths, whose extra-long proboscis can penetrate long corolla tubes to reach energy-rich nectar. In the process, they spread pollen from other flowers of the same ilk. Plant and insect have evolved together. All these flowers are pale, visible both to moths and humans. Hesperis matronalis is one of the most rewarding and easy to grow from self-saved seed.

Shady corners

Whether your garden is small or on a grand scale, there are bound to be shady corners. Sometimes these places seem like a huge challenge, occasionally insurmountable, but in actual fact they reveal all manner of wonderful opportunities. The kinds of plants that grow and thrive in these places are quite unlike many of the plants that we grow out in the open garden. They have their own special cache, their own special sort of character.

Lots of foliage plants, such as rodgersias and hostas, come into their own in spring. And in the autumn there's another opportunity for beautiful foliage plants; as the leaves all around start to fall, there's increased light and more plants will flourish.

Lots of plants that are suitable for shady corners are colonizers – plants that spread under the ground – such as wood anemones, which have these wonderful little rhizomatous roots. You will never find a wood anemone that penetrates anywhere deeper than a centimetre or two, and yet they can make huge resplendent clumps with their beautiful flowers. You can also exploit the way that

plants grow by how you propagate them. So for wood anemones, for example, you can dig up those roots during their dormant period and chop them up into little chunks a couple of centimetres long. You can either replant them in soil that you have enriched with leaf mould or gorgeous compost, or you can actually shove them into trays, into separate modules, and let them make roots and turn themselves into brand-new plants. Plant them a few centimetres apart and pretty soon you will have a whole carpet of them.

Woodruff is another plant that colonizes by galloping, as it were, across the ground, putting down little roots, and then moving on. It sends up little shoots with whorls of leaves and atop them are tiny, white flowers, bright and beautiful and fresh – as fresh as a spring morning. And the smell from them! The plant is called sweet woodruff, and was used as a strewing herb during Elizabethan times because, the moment you crush those leaves, you get this wonderful fragrance like newly mown hay. It is an ideal plant to use around other perennials, trees, or shrubs, and also bulbs that penetrate deeply into the soil, such as erythroniums and trilliums.

Opposite – Over the first few years after Neil and I had come to Glebe Cottage, my mum gave us lots of plants. Among them were four Japanese acers, including Acer palmatum *(Amoenum Group) 'Osakazuki' and* A. japonicum *'Aconitifolium'. When she brought them and we planted them together, they were small and young, now they are mature. Each time I walk through the garden, especially in autumn when 'Osakazuki' is aflame, I am reminded of her.*

Right – For me, autumn is the most atmospheric of seasons. It has its own pace, its own rhythm – contemplative and wistful. It has its own smells too, of ripe fruit, wood smoke and, mingling with them in my garden, the unexpected aroma of toffee apples emitted by one of my favourite trees, the katsura tree (Cercidiphyllum japonicum). *As its aroma begins to perfume the air, simultaneously its elegant, rounded leaves change almost imperceptibly to soft amber and pink.*

Far right – We are surrounded by deciduous trees, and during autumn all their leaves are collected into a huge heap to make leaf mould. If you have deciduous trees in or overhanging the garden, stack them in a simple container (four wooden posts hammered into the soil with wire mesh sides) or stuff them into bin liners with a few holes in the sides. The leaves will eventually turn to leaf mould. Who minds waiting, especially when you end up with such wonderful material.

Autumn woodland wonders

The garden is at its most earthy now and there is a dynamism in it that is just as powerful as it is in spring. The noise of shoots retracting, stems withering, leaves falling form a deep background rhythm as roots, tubers and bulbs draw down strength and energy into the dark, rich soil. Colour now is mellow and warm. It seeps into the consciousness inexorably – russet and amber, crimson and bronze. Chestnuts and planes, sycamores and cherries colour-wash buildings with their glowing foliage, while other parts of the garden may be set ablaze by flames of brilliant crimson created by common dogwood (*Cornus sanguinea*) in its autumn guise.

In hedges, the UK native spindle *Euonymus europaeus* is transformed from a uniform, workaday green to cerise and vivid pink. As if this were not enough, its vibrant foliage is accompanied by pink and orange fruits. As well as providing the best colour climax of the season, many spindles from more exotic climes have fascinating fruit that lasts long into autumn. Among the best for glowing, deep pink colouring is *E. planipes* or the very similar *E. sachalinensis*, both from the Far East. The European *E. latifolius* has a similar habit and stature, and its leaves also blush to brilliant red as temperatures drop and the season changes. All three of these spindles are easily accommodated in the average garden; all are slow-growing and make large shrubs rather than small trees. Any of them will light up the dull dark days of mid-autumn.

Greencombe

Joan Loraine has gardened at Greencombe, near Porlock on the north Somerset coast, UK, for more than 50 years and has created one of the most widely acclaimed woodland gardens in the world.

Case study 1

A Home from Home for Shade-Lovers

Above – The conditions at Greencombe are perfect for rhododendrons, camellias, and other acid-loving shrubs and subshrubs. Joan has four national collections, including two of the most renowned calcifuge plants: vaccinium and gaultheria. Not only is the soil acid but there is also shelter afforded by plantations of trees – oaks, hollies, and conifers. Here, Rhododendron 'Loder's White' shows just how much the conditions suit it.

Opposite – An imposing arch approached by broad, stone steps makes a dramatic entrance to the vegetable garden, with the steep, thickly wooded hillside behind. Terraced beds to either side are crammed with shady delights, while their walls are thick with ferns and primroses. Later there will be roses, wisteria, and a wealth of perennials.

GREENCOMBE WAS THE INSPIRATION for the novel *Lorna Doone*, but, long before the eponymous heroine rode across its heathery wastes, Exmoor was a forest. Much of the original forest has been felled but traces of it still persist. While there would have been no exotic rhododendrons underneath the historic oaks, Greencombe still manages to evoke feelings that a visitor might have experienced when walking around the ancient woods. There is stillness, quiet, peace. If ever a place was heaven-made for a woodland garden, Greencombe must be it. You can feel the influence of the goddess – of Mother Nature – in every mossy bank, in every ferny dell.

Porlock, on the north coast of Somerset, with the wilds of Exmoor behind it and the Bristol Channel at the foot of its north-facing slope, has a unique microclimate, long appreciated by plants and the gardeners who grow them.

"The Porlock Plantsmen", headed by Norman Hadden, were a small community of like-minded gardeners who cultivated a wide variety of unusual plants in the mid twentieth century, exchanging them and gathering together some of the most exotic and rare species ever cultivated outside in the UK. The local conditions made it possible to grow these treasures. At first glimpse, these conditions

Opposite – You could almost be in the forests of Sichuan, with its towering rhododendrons, when you come across this huge specimen of Rhododendron decorum, *one of plant hunter Robert Fortune's finds (or a hybrid from one). Its huge trusses of flowers are overwhelmingly beautiful and deliciously scented too. It clearly luxuriates in the conditions found at Greencombe.*

Right – Joan is a plantswoman of great repute. Not only does she know her plants, but, because she cultivates and grows them, her knowledge of them is intimate. Here, a special treat, Trillium grandiflorum *f.* roseum, *a rare pink form of a usually pure white flower, asks to be admired.*

Overleaf – Sometimes rhododendrons and azaleas can be truly psychedelic! Lighting plays an important part in the dramatic effects created at Greencombe as occasional sunny spotlights play on random branches. However, whatever the weather, this arrangement would still glow.

may appear unpromising: there is limited sunshine; no sun at all in some places for two of the winter months; and the aspect is exposed to northerly winds. Yet most of the weather there comes from the west, from the warm Atlantic, and many places within Porlock Bay experience no frost at all. Even though the soil is thin and acid – much of it washed down from the slopes above – it forms a ridge, a reservoir of soil on top of the shale and enables many plants to thrive. Growth is exuberant considering the soil is not rich, but then the plants get what they need – cool conditions, a moist atmosphere, and woodland soil.

Opposite – One of the most exquisite UK natives, lily of the valley, mingles with the new fronds of a charming visitor from Japan, the deliciously coloured fern Dryopteris erythrosora.

Below left – Joan holds the national collection of Polystichum setiferum, *each variety intriguing and unique. These are some of the easiest and most rewarding ferns to grow.*

Below right – Lichens and mosses abound here, thriving in the soft, moist air in the shade of the trees. The underlying feel of the garden is prehistoric, with ferns self-sporing into every crack and crevice.

Much of Joan Loraine's gardening experience was informed by the gardens of Porlock already under careful cultivation. She first saw erythroniums growing in drifts under the trees at Underway, Norman Hadden's garden, and fell in love with them. She now holds the national erythronium collection, and they throng the ground at Greencombe alongside trilliums and other choice woodlanders.

No doubt these floriferous beauties enjoy the organic regime of the garden. Many tons of leaf mould and compost are used each year to mulch and feed the woods, flowerbeds, and the thriving vegetable garden built in one of the brighter spots. The methods here are perfectly in tune with nature and are a sparkling advertisement for organic gardening. Historically, shade-loving plants got on with it on their own for aeons and were less subject to the rule of mankind, that is until the trees shading them were cut down to make way for cultivation or build ships in which to go to war on the high seas.

Above – Any plantsperson would turn green with envy at the sight of these handsome clumps of double-flowered trilliums. As most such flowers are sterile, much of the energy that would have been put into seed production is channelled into making extra petals. This is bad news for pollinating insects but means that human admirers have longer to enjoy the sight.

Opposite – Many of the foundation trees in the garden are ancient, but there is no disparity between them and the glorious array of shrubs, trees, and perennials that abound. A holly tree, most magical perhaps of all the trees native in the UK, leans over a path that lures you on through camellias, rhododendrons, and azaleas.

Throughout, the planting is artistic, bold, and imaginative. Though these 1.4ha (3½ acres) are packed with treasures from temperate woodland all around the northern hemisphere, the garden, its methods, and plants are not daunting to a beginner – rather they are encouraging. A buckler fern from Nepal will do just as well in a dark corner in Scunthorpe as at Greencombe or in its mountain home, provided it is grown sympathetically. Erythroniums, epimediums, and other shady treasures galore will all respond to being given the same conditions they enjoy at home.

The bold planting here creates a sense of adventure and romance, while wending paths reveal new vistas, though swift progress along them is impossible because of the countless horticultural treats along the way. There are scented shrubs aplenty to lift the spirits on dark winter days: *Viburnum × bodnantense* and *V. farreri*, sarcococca, mahonias, and winter-flowering honeysuckles. Both the setting and the plants at Greencombe inspire us to think that, far from being problematic, our shady areas offer exciting opportunities.

Bosvigo

Bosvigo Gardens is a series of walled gardens surrounding a Georgian house in the middle of Truro in Cornwall, UK. All the gardens are planted beautifully, but, especially in the spring, it is the woodland garden that is the most alluring. Though its creator, Wendy Perry, loves all her gardens, it is this shady retreat that she holds most dear.

Case study 2

A Magical Woodland in the Heart of the City

Above – As soon as you step foot in the garden at Bosvigo, you enter another world. Spring comes early to the southwest of the UK, and by early spring the woodland garden has launched into its vernal celebration. You are then lured by the vivid greens and dashes of pink, fresh and new and full of promise.

Opposite – A little planting of an exquisite Japanese acer, Acer palmatum *(Palmatum Group) 'Corallinum', sparkles at Bosvigo. When you get closer, you can appreciate the delicacy of this very special tree, growing as it would in its native home, by gracing the space between the canopy overhead and the woodland floor below. Both new leaves and new shoots are a perfect shade of coral-pink.*

IF YOU WERE LOOKING for a place that perfectly personified woodland plants in a setting in which they would thrive, you would probably imagine the countryside, a big rural garden, hectares of beech or oak at the edge of an amazing pastoral landscape. Yet in the midst of Truro, cathedral city of Cornwall, after turning off a suburban road, you can wander up a little path between trees and find yourself entering another reality, an enchanted wood. You forget that you are surrounded by houses, that cars and buses are travelling down the road just over the hedge. Spread out at your feet are rare Chinese epimediums and erythroniums, with their reflexed petals pulled taut, their marbled leaves infinitely patterned like the pebbled bed of a stream. There, too, you can admire the jewel-like flowers of early bulbs, strewn over the ground as though by elfin hands.

Overhead, the tracery of branches of huge, old sycamore and beech is echoed by an understorey of smaller, daintier trees, from exotic venues – the woods of Japan or the forests of Sichuan. The venerable trees stand guard protectively, sheltering the genteel newcomers/incomers as they begin to open their translucent leaves or parade the first of their pendulous catkins or strange, spidery flowers. There are dainty acers, witch hazels, corylopsis, and cornus

43

*Above – From time to time you must look up from the plants that flower at ground level, to take in the tiered branches of the pagoda tree (*Cornus alternifolia *'Argentea') or the pink butterflies of* Magnolia × loebneri *'Leonard Messel'.*

Opposite above left – Hepaticas offer a spell-binding mix of marbled leaves and clear blue flowers.

Opposite above right – The bright yellow stars and ferny foliage of Anemone ranunculoides *'Pleniflora' are interlaced here with the slender, elegant, lime-green leaves of a hosta.*

Opposite below left – Is it a polyanthus or a primrose? Whichever, it is the perfect colour to enhance the spring scene.

Opposite below right – Pale hellebores bow out to Brunnera macrophylla *'Jack Frost'.*

here, disporting themselves beside the winding paths and giving shelter in their turn to carpets of delights. Magnolias are decked with their first flowers – *M.* × *loebneri* 'Leonard Messel' in soft lilac pink and *M. stellata* in white.

Already there have been snowdrops galore, and like everything at Bosvigo they will have been the best, the most exquisite, the rare, and the special. But though you may find treasures here each time the sinuous paths take another turn, allcomers are given their due, seen to best advantage and displayed alongside other cherished riches. Overlapping with the snowdrops are eranthis, scillas, and myriad little blue-flowering bulbs. If you stoop to examine the details of these exquisite combinations, you get the feeling that everything is busy, and you are just part of the vernal hubbub. The year has yawned and stretched and now it is busy, moving forward and conjuring up confections of flower and foliage.

Everything looks so natural at Bosvigo, as if a spell from a fairy wand has brought it into being. But this garden is the labour of love of Wendy Perry, who has created it over the course of 30 years. Its "always-been-there" air belies the enormous amount of work she

Previous page – It is hardly surprising that people fall in love with delectable North American woodlanders such as Erythronium *'Joanna'. No doubt, odes would be written to them if anyone could find a rhyme for erythronium. They need a deep root run, enriched with compost or leaf mould, and after this initial cosseting should be left to their own devices.*

Opposite – Epimediums and tellimas thrive between stepping stones through a bed.

Above – Successful woodland gardening is as much about celebrating how plants self-seed as carefully choosing what to plant where. Here, primroses take full advantage of the perfect conditions.

has poured into it, both in terms of its origination and its constant maintenance and development. Nothing stays the same in a garden, and Wendy, a perfectionist through and through, constantly seeks to enhance what seems to many visitors to be perfect.

It is hard, painstaking work. On her hands and knees, swathed in her emblematic pinny, Wendy addresses the minutiae of maintaining a garden like this. In mid-winter there are also bigger jobs to do, paths to re-establish and neaten, hedges to trim, shrubs to prune, leaf mould and compost to spread, and new ideas to put into practice.

Until recently Wendy ran a nursery, and one of her obsessions was, and still is, hellebores – forms of *Helleborus* × *hybridus*. In her woodland garden they are gathered into groups according to their colours, not regimented but eased into mouthwatering combinations that make you want to go straight home and do the same thing. There are soft yellows mixed with the pale blue of *Puschkinia scilloides* var. *libanotica*, while deep crimsons and

Opposite – Muscari is immensely useful in a woodland environment. Pale blue forms such as this M. *'Jenny Robinson' are especially lovely and, even when they play second fiddle, as here with* Erythronium *'Jeanette Brickell', they are a finishing touch, adding sparkle to the arrangement.*

Below – The vertical stems of Nectaroscordum siculum *thrust rapidly upwards, promising another floral treat now that earlier bulbs have started to fizzle. Although most members of the onion clan prefer sun, this allium relative is happy in shade. Ransoms (wild garlic) are another onion that loves a shady spot. Some gardeners would shun it because of its smell, but I welcome it into my garden.*

pale pigeon-greys appear with mats of ajuga. Everything here is considered yet put together in such an authoritative way that you are never aware of the master plan.

No, master plan is not the right term, for this is a female creation, its meticulous tapestry stitched and embroidered with love and empathy. Experience has been Wendy's teacher and, even though she has very definite ideas about how she wants her garden to look, everything she does is informed by natural laws. She knows that if her plants are to reward her and create the effects she has envisaged, then she must give them what they need.

The paths at Bosvigo lead you gently up the slope, criss-crossing the site, so that you are always surrounded by the garden, in the midst of it, and the form of the plants reflects this feeling too. So many woodland plants are colonizers, making carpets, mats, and soft, repeated mounds where they have self-seeded in the deep leaf mould. You have to admire the craft and the art of Wendy's design but simultaneously acknowledge the otherworldly nature and the enchantment of the garden she has created.

Woodland plant directory

Epimedium grandiflorum 'Rose Queen'

This is one of the most beautiful and delicate of all the epimediums. It is incredibly useful in dry, shady spots. It loses all its foliage during winter but in spring up come their almost transparent, heart-shaped leaves and above them the most exquisite of pale pink flowers, with little, white, spidery insides. Easy to grow.

Colchicum

Just when you think the garden is going to sleep for autumn, out come the colchicums. Their common name is naked ladies, because they flower after the foliage has fizzled down to the ground. These great big, purple chalices come bursting through the soil, opening wide on sunny days and providing big splashes of colour in the autumn garden.

Helleborus

Hellebores have become incredibly popular during the last 20 years. They have been grown in UK gardens since Victorian times, but the range of colours and forms now available is really mind-boggling. I love the way you have to reach down and turn the flower up to see its secrets. Many are striped, while others are self-coloured.

Matteuccia struthiopteris

Shuttlecock fern (*Matteuccia struthiopteris*) is one of the most wonderful and architectural plants of early spring. It is very well named because each of its new collections of fronds looks just like a shuttlecock, which expands into marvellous, symmetrical clumps that quickly cover the ground. It is particularly good with Japanese primulas.

Arum italicum subsp. *italicum* 'Marmoratum'

This is an arum to write poems about. Its handsome, marbled leaves last all winter and fade in summer, when the green flowers, hardly noticed in the midst of the woodland garden, appear. They are followed by green berries, maturing to orange and red, on thickly clothed stems. Blackbirds love them – and so do gardeners.

Geranium nodosum

This species is perhaps the most useful of all cranesbills (*Geranium*) for a shady spot. It is evergreen and it flowers continuously from late spring right the way through until mid- or late autumn. Its gorgeous, broad, green leaves are spangled with purple flowers. In autumn the foliage takes on beautiful, red, and orange tints too. It spreads furiously.

Epimedium × rubrum

Epimedium × rubrum is so-called because its leaves are tinged with red. It is one of the best ground cover plants for a shady place. In this picture it combines with *Milium effusum* 'Aureum', a gorgeous, golden grass. The contrast between the two perennials is typical of the sort of things that you can achieve in spaces under trees or between shrubs.

Veratrum

Veratrums are much more statuesque than most woodland plants. With their broad, pleated leaves, they are extremely handsome but very, very slow growing. Eventually they will produce spikes of delightful, small flowers, in subtle shades of green and brown. An absolutely choice plant.

Polygonatum × hybridum

The graceful stems of Solomon's seal (*Polygonatum × hybridum*) used to be a familiar sight in British woodland. Now most of the plants are confined to gardens, and what a beautiful addition they are, with their tall, arching stems and twinned leaves. They really are one of the most graceful of spring's woodlanders.

Smyrnium perfoliatum

I love plants that are green right the way through, and this plant makes splashes of brilliant colour. Its flowers are halfway between lime-green and gamboge-yellow. It is a biennial and sows itself around furiously once you've got it established. It mixes and mingles with absolutely everything else.

Tellima grandiflora

This American plant has become a common sight in British gardens. Many Americans think of it as a weed, but I adore its tall spires with tiny, fringed flowers. The foliage is wonderful too. Like many small, green flowers, tellima's blooms are fragrant, to attract insects, which might otherwise prefer bigger and more beautiful flowers.

Narcissus poeticus var. *recurvus*

No wonder Narcissus fell in love with his own reflection and was changed into this beautiful flower. This is one of the last of all the daffodils to flower and it is worth waiting for. It has sensational scent too, and the simplicity of these beautiful, white flowers with their short, green-yellow cups ringed in red is just out of this world.

Erythronium californicum 'White Beauty'

Almost all trout lilies (*Erythronium*) are north American, and there they carpet woodlands with their graceful, reflexed flowers. They are easy enough to establish in UK gardens, but because they make very deep roots, you must plant them deeply and give them fairly lush growing conditions.

Paeonia 'Late Windflower'

This is a selection from Beth Chatto. It has a unique purity and simplicity. Tall stems with single, white flowers rise above fresh green foliage. Later on, the foliage is tinged with red and russet, so the plant stays looking wonderful far past its flowering and late into autumn. It is easy to grow and long-lived once established. It loves dappled shade.

Cyclamen hederifolium Silver-Leaved Group

In the early rainy days of autumn, the first flowers of this cyclamen appear. There can be masses of these tiny, graceful flowers with their reflexed petals. As the flowers fade, the leaf stems spiral to the ground, carrying the seeds down to be taken by ants and create new colonies. Each *C. hederifolium* has unique foliage.

Primula vulgaris

Despite its ubiquity, everybody treasures primroses (*Primula vulgaris*). Their pale yellow flowers with deep egg-yolk centres and pink stems are the glory of spring. In a garden setting they introduce an informality, and they spread wonderfully by seed. You can also divide them during late summer, as the flowers begin to fade.

Convallaria majalis 'Fortin's Giant'

Lily of the valley (*Convallaria majalis*) always reminds me of my childhood, as we had oceans of it in a bed that ran along the side of our house. It never saw sunlight, but each spring we'd gather bunches of the flowers and bring them into the house. Its scent is its real attraction, even though the flowers are pristine and the leaves perfect.

Galanthus nivalis

As soon as one snowdrop (*Galanthus nivalis*) opens, we are convinced that spring is on its way. The bulbs proliferate both by spontaneously dividing and by setting seed. It only takes two or three years for seeds to become fresh flowering bulbs. Plant snowdrops in drifts and divide every few years. Replant the bulbs singly and in a nice random fashion.

Ranunculus ficaria 'Brazen Hussy'

Christopher Lloyd first found this plant in the woods near his garden at Great Dixter, in the UK, and brought it back home. Since then it has become one of the most popular cultivars, with its polished, bronze leaves. When the sun shines, the flowers open wide, their yellow petals gloriously lacquered and shiny. They really are one of the sights of spring.

Anemone hybrida 'White Queen'

As the leaves fall in autumn, there is another opportunity for beautiful plants to be in the limelight. All Japanese anemones flower at this season on tall stems, perhaps to compete with other foliage that has grown up over the summer. This variety has almost semi-double flowers and yet offers wonderful pollen and nectar treats to insects.

Galium odoratum

I have used sweet woodruff (*Galium odoratum*) countless times in my garden. It is very accommodating, but it best loves the shady places under trees. It is a plant small of stature but big in personality, easy to propagate by digging up the whole thing, pulling it apart and planting each piece separately with some good leaf mould.

Digitalis purpurea f. albiflora

In wild populations of foxgloves (*Digitalis*) you sometimes see swathes of this exquisite, white variety. It is the one I love best, and it is the easiest to grow in a garden setting because not only does it blend well with absolutely everything, but it also looks particularly good in a shady place. I think white flowers always look best in the shade anyway.

Maianthemum racemosum

This North American woodlander, known to many as smilacina, bears tiny, creamy white flowers with a beautiful scent. It is closely related to polygonatum and convallaria, and loves the same conditions: deep woodland soil. Even if you live in a town or city, you can give these plants exactly that by planting them with a big load of leaf mould.

Ajuga reptans 'Pink Surprise'

Bugles (*Ajuga*) make some of the very best of ground cover plants. Their growth is dense and handsome but they do not prevent anything else from coming through. They are perfect around bulbs. In spring they come into their own, when these tall spires of usually blue, but in this case pink, flowers burst on the scene, providing food for early pollinators.

Hyacinthoides non-scripta

What would British woodlands be like without English bluebells (*Hyacinthoides non-scripta*) in mid- and late spring? Their continuous colour reaches into the distance and dispels all evidence of horizons. Even in a small garden, bluebells can be a springtime treat. Beware, though, they spread rapidly, as do the even more vigorous Spanish bluebells.

Jeffersonia dubia

This plant tugs at your heartstrings. A typical Cinderella plant, it shoots to stardom when its flowers and exquisite leaves tinged with pink and scarlet appear but quickly fade after a few weeks. Take care to mark where it is planted, otherwise you are liable to dig it out during summer and replace it with something much more mundane. It really is a treasure.

Omphalodes cappadocica 'Cherry Ingram'

Navelworts (*Omphalodes*) are so-called because of the lovely, dimpled centres to their beautiful, brilliant blue flowers. Although this low-growing plant is only a few centimetres tall, it has great presence and makes pools of blue in the shade. Basal cuttings taken in spring should root successfully in gritty compost.

Campanula latifolia

This British native can be seen up and down the UK countryside but particularly in the north at the edge of woodland or in hedgerows. It loves dappled shade, and each clump lasts for years, making tall spikes up to 1m (3ft) in height. This is one of the most handsome of late summer-flowering plants, ideal in shady spots. Very tolerant and easy to grow.

Pulmonaria saccharata

Lungwort (*Pulmonaria*) is so-called because medieval herbalists used it to treat lung disease and respiratory complaints. Its foliage is its finest feature, often dappled and splattered with white. In some forms the leaves are entirely silver. It has lots of nicknames – "Joseph and Mary", "soldiers and sailors" – because its flowers can change from blue to pink.

Anemone nemorosa 'Allenii'

This is a very desirable, pale blue-grey form of the UK native wood anemone (*Anemone nemorosa*). Even though they look the most fragile of plants, they are toughies and can withstand anything. They will colonize the ground quickly. To see their beautiful flowers following the sun on a spring day is a real joy. Would that I had time to watch them all day.

Trillium chloropetalum and T. grandiflorum

Dark, almost reptilian-looking *T. chloropetalum* growing beside the immaculate pure whiteness of *T. grandiflorum* is at once dramatic and humorous. Both require a deep rich root run. Although expensive, it is advisable to buy trilliums in flower to see exactly what you've got and ensure the plant is of flowering size.

Aconitum carmichaelii

All monkshoods (*Aconitum*) have a dangerous air. Although they are all extremely poisonous, in terms of finding something for the autumn woodland garden which will add depth of colour and stature nothing beats them. You can propagate them very easily by division in spring. Make sure you wash your hands afterwards though.

Geranium phaeum

Although the flowers of mourning widow (*Geranium phaeum*) are typically very dark, they do not get lost in the spring garden because they appear very early. Each plant is smothered in flowers, and its foliage, with its near-black splodges, is handsome for months. Cut it back hard after flowering and it will make wonderful dense tufts.

Meconopsis Fertile Blue Group 'Lingholm'

Not surprisingly, Himalayan blue poppies (*Meconopsis*) are the holy grail of many a gardener. If your soil is on the acid side and you can offer light shade and shelter, you may succeed. 'Lingholm' belongs to the perennial *M. grandis* group but can be grown from seed – unlike many of its ilk, which need to be divided.

Scilla siberica

Siberian squill (*Scilla siberica*) is one of spring's easiest bulbs, and one of the jolliest too. The bulbs are quite large and produce several spikes of flowers, but the flower stems themselves are never more than 15cm (6in) tall. It will seed itself profusely, and the bulbs will also divide, so pretty soon you will have a big patch of blue.

seaside

On pebble beaches, the round seeds of sea kale roll until they meet some obstacle, a big stone perhaps. Then, provided there is adequate fresh water and some semblance of soil, they will germinate and add to the colony. The almost lunar landscape created by their low mounds among the endless shingle is a study in pattern and texture within a minimal colour palette.

- - - - - - - - - - - - - - - - - - - -

Along the Beach & on the Shore

Opposite – Texture, form, and touch are all-important in seaside plantings, even when they are uncomfortable! Lots of plants that thrive in seaside settings have armaments, and many make rosettes. This unusual thistle is a biennial, producing typical, purple flowers, but it is most exciting at this stage, when its long, cruel leaves are outlined and veined with silver.

IF YOUR GARDEN lies by the sea or if you are out of earshot of the sound of crashing waves and tumbling pebbles but nonetheless experience similar conditions to those you would on the shore, gardening holds many challenges. As with every other situation, though, it is a question of embracing the special qualities of the site and making the most of them, rather than struggling to do battle and impose your will on nature. If your soil is thin and gravelly and the site unsheltered and exposed, then seaside-like conditions prevail. You may not be able to taste salt in the air, but the same natural laws of the shore apply and the same plants will thrive.

Most gardening projects require soil fertility to be improved with the addition of copious amounts of organic matter. In seaside conditions, the objective is the opposite. Grit or even gravel can be incorporated by the bucketful. Results are twofold: soil fertility is reduced, and drainage enhanced. Always try to use locally sourced material both to mix with the soil and to use as a mulch.

One of the unsung pleasures of seaside holidays is experiencing new plants: rock samphire (*Crithmum maritimum*), which softens the edges of tumbled rocks with its mounds of feathery growth, or the clouds of tiny, honey-scented, white flowers hovering over the wavy, succulent leaves of sea kale (*Crambe maritima*). Such scenes

Above – A particularly blue form of Eryngium bourgatii *takes pride of place at the end of the raised bed that forms the backdrop to our seaside garden at Glebe Cottage. It is underpinned by* Erigeron karvinskianus. *Both revel in the poor, dry soil and, above all, in the sunshine, as they are in full light all day.*

Opposite – Eryngium maritimum *is the true sea holly, difficult to grow unless in pure sand. It embodies everything a true seaside plant should be. A thick, waxy coating protects its leaves from salt, sun, and wind, and sharp spines arm both leaves and the ring of bracts surrounding the flower cones against the predations of animals. Here it grows alongside restharrow.*

provide the inspiration to guide us. These are the sorts of plants that will not only help us to create the feel we aspire to but will also feel completely at home, as they thrive in coastal conditions.

Wherever they grow, plants have evolved with their environment, adapting to the prevailing conditions. Coastal plants need to be tough. They are exposed to squally winds and baking sun. They grow in sand or shingle, with little or no access to soil. Often they have taproots that plunge deep into the sand to search for nutrients and fresh water and, simultaneously, moor them to the shore. In our gardens they employ the same techniques, and, although there may be little need in an inland garden to guard against being swept away, the ability to withstand drought is an important attribute for any plant in an area with sharp drainage and poor soil.

When placing plants, emulate what happens naturally – perhaps a mother plant with her progeny close by, seeded among the shingle. Several members of the pea family flourish in maritime conditions. Restharrow carpets dunes around the UK coast, and its spangle of pink flowers are highly perfumed to attract pollinating insects.

Opposite – Sempervivums lend themselves to playing pattern games and increase so rapidly you soon have enough to make new arrangements by taking offsets and transferring them to a new site. They need no soil.

Below left – The airy-fairy, fine filigree of Artemisia schmidtiana *'Nana' is perfect besides the spherical rosettes of this sempervivum, making them look all the more globose. Colour difference sharpens the contrast too.*

Below right – Spider's web sempervivums, such as this S. arachnoideum, *surround the bold, succulent spikes of the agave.*

Powerful plant patterns

The abstract patterns that plants create – the spiral of a sempervivum, the extraordinary markings on euphorbia leaves when viewed from above – are unexpected yet deeply reassuring. When echiums crowd together to produce three-dimensional tessellations imbued with colour and texture, the plant world becomes an expression of a horticultural universe and opens up infinite possibilities to us gardeners. We can exploit these elements of pattern to our own ends. Sometimes they can be regimented: sempervivums contained within strict boundaries; grasses disciplined in identical containers to make deliberate motifs. At other times we can let them have their way, developing organically. The element of pattern underlies so much in our designs but is ever-present within the plants themselves. It is a powerful force contained within all we do, whether deliberate or accidental.

Below – Both hardy sempervivums and tender echeveria grow in the same way, expanding widthways by adding rosettes. Once you have insinuated a few rosettes between stones, they will spread exponentially, taking up residence in every crack and crevice they reach.

Succulents by the seaside

A plant living in a hot, dry place and/or a habitat in which drainage is sharp any rain that does fall quickly runs away must make use of that rain straight away or find a way of storing it. Many plants, therefore, develop foliage that, while having in-built protection from harsh, burning sunlight for the cuticle of their leaves, simultaneously store water in those leaves to make use of it when times get hard.

Sometimes the scale of their succulent leaves is vast – some of the huge agaves of the Mexican deserts have thick, fleshy leaves – while, in complete contrast, the native UK stonecrop (*Sedum acre*) has literally thousands and thousands of tiny leaves. Each one has an individual water supply that can even help that leaf become a new plant and establish an independent existence when it is separated from its parent plant. This stonecrop produces bright yellow, star-like flowers and is one of the main constituents of most proprietary green roof products.

In most cases, the surface of succulent leaves is tough and thick, but sometimes it is waxy. The texture, too, is part of the fascination. Succulents can be armed to the teeth to protect their leaves and ensure that they, rather than a passing animal or a thirsty bird, derive the advantage from their water-storage mechanism. Cacti are among the most notoriously prickly of reservoir plants – yuccas too – but use of these brilliant mechanisms is not confined to such plants from the American continent. African aloes and euphorbias from many parts of the world are heavily armoured too.

Opposite – The methods plants have evolved to store water are a constant source of wonder. The fleshy, petal-like leaves of some succulents act as reservoirs (above left), while the thick, water-filled leaves of an agave (above right) are heavily armed to prevent any opportunistic herbivore stealing a drink. Sometimes both strategies are combined (below left). Each aeonium leaf stores water until overtaken by new growth (below right).

Aeoniums are some of the most sought-after of all these succulent-leaved plants, especially the dark-leaved forms such as *A.* 'Zwartkop' – the one that is most usually grown, with its arresting rosettes of rich, dark crimson leaves, sometimes verging on the black. *Aeonium arboretum* is from the Canary Islands and is tender, but there are a host of tough perennials with succulent leaves that thrive in seaside conditions. Another exciting dark-leaved succulent is *Sedum* 'Purple Emperor', growing to 45cm (18in) tall, with its plum-coloured stems and foliage and flat heads of crimson flowers.

Above – In a corner of our seaside garden at Glebe Cottage, recently planted sea kale (grey leaves at the bottom of the picture) is doing very bravely surrounded by well-established visitors to the shore: Eryngium bourgatii, *the sword-like leaves of* Gladiolus papilio Purpureoauratus Group, and knautia. *Meanwhile,* Elaeagnus 'Quicksilver' *overlooks the scene.*

Opposite above – Sometimes you do not want the flowers of sea kale to open, the more to enjoy its special foliage. Inevitably they do and then all you can think of is how pretty they look and what a delight their honeyed perfume is on a sunny day.

Opposite below – Sea kale can be planted with the minimum of fuss.

Striking sea kales

One of the most exciting plants anyone could grow in a seaside garden is sea kale (*Crambe maritima*). In early spring, crinkled tufts of indigo-purple push their way up through the shingle at the end of last year's corky stems. Rapidly they open, the most frilly of all leaves, into a ground-hugging rosette. Their colour gradually bleaches to glaucous grey-blue, their leaves becoming thicker and more succulent. Both the surface and the shape of the leaves are designed to channel moisture into the centre of the plant. Sea kale flowers form clouds of white, headily honey scented, and they are followed by branching seedheads smothered in stone-coloured beads.

Sea kale is indigenous to the British Isles, distributed along many shingle beaches, especially in the south and east. It lives just above the high-water line and sends its strong taproots down through the loose pebbles to anchor itself firmly. Sometimes, after a particularly violent high tide has washed away the surrounding shingle, roots a metre or so long are exposed – yet the plant survives.

In gardens, these taproots are perfect material for root cuttings, and this is the best way to make new plants. The plant need not be lifted; dig down around its perimeter to expose one or two strong roots the thickness of a pencil, sever them from the main root, cut them into 3cm (1in) shoots, and plunge them to the hilt in pots or trays filled with an open mixture of loam-based compost and liberal amounts of grit. Ensure they are the right way up. Water thoroughly once and keep them in a warm, bright position. The imperative need of sea kale is sun. They will simply refuse to grow true to character if they are made to endure shady conditions. In a good year, seed may ripen well, providing another source of new plants.

In a bright, sunny, gravel garden, nothing can beat sea kale's big, silvery rosettes. It is a strong, chunky plant that is excellent anywhere its sculptured hemispheres can make a strong architectural statement. For maximum impact, grow it close to purple or magenta roses, whose colour enhances its purplish cast, or simply plant it on its own among sun-baked gravel with a sprinkling of orange eschscholzia, à la Derek Jarman.

Previous page – Eryngium maritimum, *growing among marram grass on the shore dunes, tells the story of conditions in the Cornish cove of Mount's Bay. Buffeted by sea and gale-force winds, in bright light and completely exposed, the plants on both mount and shore need to be tough.*

Opposite, below left, and below right – Three superb sea hollies: Eryngium planum *(left), a multiheaded species with an informal look;* E. variifolium *(below left), whose basal leaves are rounded, while its caulescent leaves are spiky; and* E. bourgatii *(below right), a particularly good blue form, being marked with a ribbon for seed collection later on.*

Sea hollies in their element

Sea hollies (*Eryngium*) are much lauded and rightly so. Despite their common name, the vast majority recommended for our gardens are from the mountains of Europe and Turkish Asia. Species such as *E. bourgatii* thrive in hot, dry conditions. The midribs and veins of its spiky basal foliage are picked out in silvery white, giving it a shimmery effect. In the best forms, the silvery green flowers with their large bracts turn gradually to the deepest blue. Charismatic *E. alpinum* has a lacy ruff around its flowers. They are a rich, true blue, and although the plant gives the impression of being heavily armed, it is, in fact, soft to the touch. *Eryngium maritimum* is the true sea holly, difficult to grow unless in pure sand. Its foliage and flowers are extremely spiky. When ready to be pollinated, the silver flowers turn bright blue. One biennial sea holly is especially valued for its ornamental qualities: Miss Willmott's ghost (*E. giganteum*). Once you have it, it will haunt your garden forever.

Material matters

For me, and for the vast majority of gardeners, the most important materials we use in our gardens are living materials – plants. But to conjure the atmosphere of a place or rather to build on what is already there, to emphasize it, and make its ambience all-pervading is a vital part of creating a garden. Hard landscaping and design must be supportive but, especially in a modestly sized garden, the materials must be sympathetic with the overall ethos and planting. The smaller a garden is, the more essential it is for elements within it never to jar or work against the intended design.

The way materials work with plants, setting them off and providing a framework, is crucial. In our gardens we do not want to be constantly aware of what grade of gravel, what size of pebbles, what quirky rusty artefacts there are. We prefer to concentrate on the plants, the shape of a santolina, the way an osteospermum creeps out through the shingle and opens its big daisies to the sun.

In any garden the use of local materials is imperative. The idea of the vernacular, of the whole place having grown up organically, is of central importance. In a seaside garden, whether it is within sight and sound of the sea or far from it, old railway sleepers or floorboards work brilliantly well with shingle or pebbles. They provide a change in texture and in pace as you walk around the space. But they need to look sea-washed and weather-beaten, not mossy and damp.

At Glebe Cottage, in one corner, protected by the dry-stone wall, is a long raised bed, at the front of which is a huge stone. Its top is about 1m (3ft) square and it is perhaps 30cm (1ft) deep – perfect for lounging about in the sun, which is exactly what my mum used it for. It was my mum's inspiration in imbuing the whole place with a relaxed holiday air that was responsible for the bed being called the seaside garden. There we have created the atmosphere of the seaside without employing obvious tactics – there's not an old anchor or a lobster pot in sight. Principally it is the plants themselves that conjure up the sound of crashing waves. Familiar plants of cliff face and shingle shore are bound to do well in a position such as this. They not only thrive here but also look the part in this sun-baked corner.

Below – Every few years, we take our seaside garden to pieces, remove all the stones from the surface, lift plants that have become too invasive, and replant. The pebbles are all returned. It is difficult to make them look convincingly natural – though essential to try. You should not even be aware of them when admiring the plants.

Opposite – Materials and "props" should always be sympathetic. Gabions (above left) can be useful for retaining or background walls, while the texture of the pebbles they contain provides visual interest and organic forms within a symmetrical structure. An old propeller (above right) adds a nautical detail, while old iron and bleached wood (below right) always seem to fit. Railway sleepers (below left) make a sturdy path over ballast.

The power of pots

Containers are fun. Not only do they give instant gratification, which is unusual in gardening, but their contents can be changed whenever the gardener decides. This can be particularly important in a small garden and for those with just a courtyard, patio, or a window ledge. Container growing encourages everyone to have a go, regardless of their expertise, and experimentation is easy. Use well-drained potting compost with a high loam content, to maintain slow but sturdy growth.

The containers themselves should fit the seaside context. Simplicity is the key both for container and plants. One of the best ideas is to find decorative pots that can accommodate black plastic pots inside them without their showing. This way, when plants are decidedly past their best, another arrangement can be dropped into the limelight. Try using large, plain terracotta pots or galvanized buckets. Regroup pots occasionally to create a brand-new display. Above all, be adventurous and have fun.

Chygurno

After leaving the Moule family house in Southern Cornwall, steps take you from one level to another, joining horizontal paths that lead you on level walks between beds on one side and the steep landscape below on the other. Despite the gradient, every centimetre of earth is covered by vegetation. Plants that spread and make themselves at home are particularly welcome here. Materials are always natural, always local.

Case study 3

Making a Virtue of Steep Cliffs & Bare Rocks

Above – The light here is clear and pure, and the colouring is vivid. Crocosmias and agapanthus, two of the iconic plants of this garden, demonstrate the clarity of the light with their brilliant red and deep blue flowers.

Opposite – Many would find the gardens at Chygurno idyllic; they overlook the sea and a headland across the cove. The silhouette of the Scots pine is enough to illustrate just how exposed and blown about it can be. The landscape and the conditions here are in control. They shape the garden, and it is obvious that the owners acknowledge the power of the site and the elements that affect the garden and go along with them.

IN THE UK, WE LIVE ON AN ISLAND, several islands in fact, and our coastline is gloriously varied and rich in its landscape. Gardening by the sea can present many problems and a multitude of solutions. Even when a garden is on level ground, there are still salt-laden gales, lack of shelter, paucity of soil – in fact, sometimes no soil at all – to contend with. But so much of the UK coastline is very different and far from flat; it can be rugged, almost mountainous, with precipitous cliffs tumbling down into the sea, bare rock, and sheer drops that would challenge even the most intrepid ibex, let alone a gardener.

One such place is at Chygurno, in southern Cornwall, UK, where 15 years ago Robert and Carol Moule took on 1.2ha (3 acres) of steep, overgrown terrain and transformed them into what has become a stunning, vertical garden. Though there are a few plateaux, usually in the form of a level path before a steep drop to another level, the whole garden is about descent and ascent!

On the journey down or up, there are views of the cove, framed by exotic species of shrubs and perennials, many of which would need protection in most gardens. Here, under the influence of the sea and the south-facing aspect, plants from South Africa and the Antipodes, which many of us might consider out of the question, do

79

Opposite – Steps and walls look as though they have almost grown out of the landscape. They are organic, uncontrived, yet guide you through and around the garden. You are led this way and that, experiencing surprises close at hand – as with this bank of brilliant red crocosmia.

Below left – The acid, lime-green euphorbia against the brilliant vermilion of Crocosmia *'Lucifer' sets up a retina-searing contrast.*

Below right – Contrasts in colour but also in form give verve and dynamism to the plantings. Here, two bronze cordylines thrust through clumps of crocosmia.

not just survive but flourish. These are not only the usual suspects that many of us might try in our own gardens, such as agapanthus and crocosmia, but also proteas and restios, which would struggle in most situations in the UK. Agaves and aeoniums that need shelter from frost can be left outside to fend for themselves. It does not feel like "outside" for them; there is none of the self-consciousness of having aeoniums at Glebe Cottage in pots by the front door!

To say that the garden is dramatic would be to understate the case. There are familiar elements – the garden has a true Cornish feel – but there is an exotic undercurrent, something unexpected and sometimes perhaps unsettling, but always exciting.

Near the entrance to the garden are man-made walls festooned by self-seeders and neat evergreens. This theme continues around the front of the house, where, perched high above the cove but now exposed to full sun and the full force of the weather, plants that revel in such conditions can wend their own way among the rocks.

Yet there are also the familiar rhododendrons and camellias that we expect to see in the southwest of the UK, and in among them in spring are bluebells galore carpeting the woods. Having zigzagged to the foot of the garden, the visitor encounters tree ferns, bananas, isoplexis, and cannas – a veritable jungle revelling in the soft, warm air and out of the way of gale and tempest.

The garden at Chygurno seems to have grown out of the granite organically, and this effect is enhanced by self-seeding plants. These are encouraged to insinuate themselves around shrubs and larger perennials. Meanwhile, grasses such as *Stipa tenuissima*, with its soft, wafty fronds, lend a misty air and provide contrast against the hard, grey stone. Equally, gangs of crocosmia in vivid vermilion and sizzling orange run riot, filling any available soil with their joyful blooms and verdant foliage. When introduced in the 1880s, montbretia (*C.* × *crocosmiiflora*) was hailed as a wonderful, new ornament for gardens. Now an outcast from gardens because of its colonizing habit, it has made its way to cliffs, hedgerows, and road verges, especially along the south coasts of England and Ireland.

Above – Walls, steps, and terrace, even the seat and trough, blend seamlessly. Their purpose is not to be admired as hard landscaping in their own right, but to do a job. Because they are built with whatever is to hand and with love and understanding of the place, they are beautiful and just perfect.

Opposite above – Low perennials and evergreens frame the view of the sea, echoing the shapes of the rocks and the promontory across the water.

Opposite below – Erigeron karvinskianus is in complete control. Even though it is from Mexico, this little, wall-hugging daisy is a perfect match for the Cornish granite.

Many people regard it as a nuisance just because it is so prolific but, at Chygurno, montbretia and other crocosmias are welcomed.

Recently, crocosmias have had something of a renaissance, fitting in with modern styles of planting. Old varieties have been resuscitated and new cultivars created. As the summer progresses, they supply an injection of hot colour that gets the garden pulse racing, and they make ideal plants growing among the rocks here at Chygurno, a reprise of their natural habitat where they flourish on mountainsides – often among boulders.

Within this seaside garden, there are several different habitats, but the garden's success can be attributed to its owners recognizing this and celebrating it. Areas do not end abruptly; they flow into each other, down the hillside. The garden rejoices in what it can grow and the differences and contrasts between the series of scenarios that the site suggests. There is much to be gleaned from the practices here, though it is unlikely that many of us would be lucky enough to share so many scenarios. Nonetheless, there are aspects that are relevant to many of us and we can all take inspiration.

Solent Cottage

Solent Cottage

The garden here, at Solent Cottage in Hampshire, UK, is celebratory. It relishes in its situation, homing in on the plants that love to live beside the sea, and making imaginative use of all the treasures that the sea pitches onto the beach.

Case study 4

The Ultimate Pebble Garden

Above – The garden, sea, and sky – a sense of infinity – are grounded on the beach. The garden accepts it is part of the beach and is happy. The plants that grow there can be themselves; they are true to character, shaped by gales and sea spray, and in their element.

Opposite – The plants seem to have arrived, communed, and decided where they are going to live. They huddle together on days when the gales blow, and drink in the warmth of a shimmering sun, enjoying the heat reflected by the shingle. Though the garden is rich in artefacts, they are no more contrived than the planting and enhance it perfectly.

IF YOUR GARDEN lies by the sea or it experiences maritime conditions, there are many challenges. As with every other situation, it is a question of embracing the specialness of the site rather than entering into the fray and trying to combat the conditions and impose an antipathetic will. Perhaps seaside plants, together with those from moor and mountain, display the widest variety of adaptations to their living conditions, honed over thousands, often millions, of years.

The back garden at Solent Cottage, Hampshire, UK, has no real boundaries unless you count the beach and the sea, but the shore, the ocean, the sky are constantly changing, providing a mutable background to the garden's cycles and initiating its moods. You do not have to imagine the sound of crashing waves or receding pebbles, rolling backwards and tossed forward by their force – it is here.

There is no attempt to control nature, no clash or awkwardness, no feeling of restraint or restriction. Hummocks of santolina, rosemary, lavender, and helichrysum huddle together and occasionally explode into growth, establishing subtle rhythms among the shingle. These are plants of the Provençal maquis, of the dry slopes that tumble down to Mediterranean shores. All have skinny, needle-like leaves that cut down transpiration. Droughty

*Right – There are more members in the daisy family (Asteraceae) than in any other flowering plant family. Some of them have evolved to thrive in maritime conditions and always look the part among driftwood and shingle, where they spread out to make broad mats starred with their pretty flowers. This is Californian beach aster (*Erigeron glaucus*).*

Far right – "Mezzies" – or mesembryanthemums – hale from South Africa, but thrive beside the sea in southern England. Their tiny, succulent leaves act as a reservoir, storing water for needy times. They stay all winter and tiny pieces will take root easily, but it is their daisy flowers in sizzling colours that make such scintillating splashes among the predominant silvers and grey-greens.

Opposite – With plants scrambling and colonizing, edges are blurred – is it a path or is it the beach? As long as you can wander through the plants, enjoying the perfume of their flowers and the scent of aromatic oils released by their foliage, what does it matter? Drink in the ozone, and revel in the seaside experience.

Overleaf – Like fire beacons standing proud throughout the garden, these kniphofias appear to live up to their name of red hot poker. These are South African plants, and most prefer adequate moisture at their roots for at least part of the year. Perhaps deep under this shingle is rich clay, which their roots can penetrate.

conditions frequently experienced on the Hampshire coast present no problems, and, during winter, drainage is sharp enough for plants not to drown nor even have to paddle. Many other plants here, including the UK-indigenous *Crambe maritima*, have a waxy coating to their leaves or are covered in fine fur or hair to protect the cuticle of the leaf from the blazing sun and salty winds.

At Solent Cottage, the gravel of the beach extends to cover and create the paths – you are literally walking on the beach. In some places, pebbles are underlaid with permeable membrane, an artifice invisible to the visitor but one that retains moisture and cuts down on seedling weeds. Having said that, though, self-seeded adventurers are encouraged to set up home, and if liable to be trodden on or damaged, they are are moved surreptitiously to safer places where they blend in perfectly. Meanwhile, annuals, marigolds, and sweet alyssum insinuate themselves at the paths' edges like a crowd of onlookers at a royal parade.

Liz Shackleton designs textiles, and her artistic bent manifests itself throughout the Solent Cottage garden in its various structures and quirky constructions. Many are *objets trouvés*, revelling in the fact that they have become weather-beaten, perhaps distorted or seen now as beautiful things in their own right, away from their original function of hinge or machine part, of wheel or spar.

Such artless arrangements of driftwood and beach salvage, seemingly just washed up on the last high tide, are used not only

Opposite and below – Driftwood, old iron, and the skeletal remains of maritime structures (opposite) all furnish the garden, their weather-worn, sometimes rusty surfaces being the perfect accompaniment to silver and grey foliage. Equally, such artefacts provide a fitting foil for the soft pink flowers of this rugosa rose (below) and its sealing-wax-red hips and amber autumn foliage, which will follow.

ornamentally but also to do a job of work. They retain groups of plants or create short, random, hotchpotch fences that both protect plants and supply an element of definition, low-level architecture, to the scene. Such little barriers work brilliantly.

There are no hedges as such at Solent Cottage; instead, a wealth of shrubs decorate the beds and hint that boundaries might exist. All are well chosen, belying their random presence, and all are apt. There is *Eleagnus × ebbingei* – noted and oft-used for its ability always to look pukka – coping uncomplainingly with gales and salt spray thanks to its leathery leaves. Making light of the conditions in a different way, *Lotus hirsutus*, which goes under the common name of hairy Canary clover (thank goodness it has a capital "C"), is covered in fine hairs, which shrug off windy, saline conditions. In an inland garden subject to winter wet and freezing temperatures, plants such as lotus, coronilla, and tree lupins – a trio of peas, all leguminous – might succumb, but here at Solent Cottage, with its brilliant drainage and relatively high winter temperatures, there are no such problems.

Colours in this seaside garden are either soft and shimmery, as in the case of much of the foliage on helichrysum, lavender, santolina, and their ilk, or they are vivid and obvious, like so many of the unapologetic magenta flowers of some varieties of *Rosa rugosa* (see p.85) and lampranthus or the fiery hues of red hot pokers and calendula. The flower colours sing out and occasionally shout out loud, enhanced by the neutral backdrop of stone, driftwood, and the subtly changing but usually subdued hues of the sea and sky. Occasionally, though, stormy weather sets in, and the garden is forgotten.

The archetype of a beach garden is that of Derek Jarman's Prospect Cottage on the shingle at Dungeness, Kent, UK, where the film director salvaged driftwood, scrap metal, and debris that had been tossed onto the beach. Both his garden and the one at Solent Cottage go with the flow, embracing the conditions, never fighting against them. However, there was always something melancholy or at least pensive about Jarman's garden, while the Solent Cottage garden is a light-hearted, cheerful sort of a place.

St Michael's Mount

The Aubyn family home, built on an
island that was once a mound surrounded
by farmland and the site of a medieval
priory, dominates Mount's Bay across the
water from Marazion, close to Penzance,
in Cornwall, UK.

Case study 5

Surrounded by Sea, an Island Garden

Above – Not so much seaside as sea-surrounded, the majestic gardens and castle of St Michael's Mount become even more monumental in splendid isolation when the tide is in, as here. This is seaside gardening on a grand scale. Could it be more impressive or awe-inspiring?

Opposite – Even the towering steeples of echium and the impressive jet bursts of palm and cordyline foliage are dwarfed by the towering turrets of the castle. The overriding green of subtropical leaves with big splashes of red, here from the bunched flowers of embothrium and grevillea, become all the more organic when contrasted with the granite grey of the fortifications above.

THERE ARE NOT MANY seaside gardens on the scale of St Michael's Mount. In fact, it is unique – an island in the middle of Mount's Bay with all the features and feeling of a wild island, yet which is a consummate garden, every rock, every crevice playing its part in a magnificent celebration of this extraordinary place.

Frost is seldom a problem in true seaside gardens, although for some of us gardening inland in the UK under similar conditions – thin, stony soils, lack of water, and high exposure – winter temperatures may plummet way below freezing. Not so on St Michael's Mount. Many of the plants that most of us are obliged to dash under cover at the first signs of autumnal cold are permanent residents, with no winter retreats provided and none needed. Though it is warm here, it is not always tranquil. Winter gales subject the isle to a lashing, and salt spray drenches its almost perpendicular faces and its terraces, which give access to most parts of the slopes.

The sea does not lap at the shore – there are no shores – and, even though at low tide the causeway that joins St Michael's Mount to the mainland is exposed, it serves to remind just how unpredictable the sea can be. At one time, probably around 1500 BC, the mount was many kilometres inland, and for thousands of years before

Above – The statuesque rosettes of Furcraea parmentieri *almost distract your attention from the magnificent views of the ocean, but the plant's very nature reminds you that this is an extraordinary place, capable of transporting you mentally to other climes, new realities. Everywhere you look, there are new plants to discover and fresh experiences to enjoy.*

Opposite – Agaves, succulents, and cistus cling to the cliff face, each exploiting its own niche in the rocks. Surely one of the qualifications for gardening on St Michael's Mount must be the ability to abseil. Dealing with such sharp and dangerous leaves has to be a hazardous business – not for the armchair gardener.

that leaves must have rotted and soil been left on the "rock in the forest". So, although this great rock, which gathers heat and stores it, is incontestably a huge lump of granite, it does boast deposits of wonderfully fertile soil.

It is the steepness of the site, the geography and geology of the mount, that dictate not only what is grown but also how it can be gardened. And the climate and weather play a major part too. Having taken for granted for years that plants would automatically survive, the gardeners here had to think again after a couple of harsh winters and extraordinarily stormy months. Succulents that had lived for years were lost, and other plants took a battering. They have been replaced, in some cases, by hardier inhabitants or those most likely to survive if there are repeat performances of extreme conditions.

Those who work in the gardens are an extraordinary breed – very special people who adore the work they do. This is unusual type of work. On the steep, almost vertical faces of some parts of the garden, it is not so much spadework as ropework that is involved. Sometimes the gardeners are suspended from ropes when they put in new plants

95

Previous page – Does the blue of the agapanthus make the sea look more blue or is it the other way round? Agapanthus are plants of the mountains; they always look right in the midst of stony outcrops but somehow lend themselves to a maritime setting. What's more, they thrive in such conditions, enjoying the clear light and the mild temperatures.

Below and opposite – So much of the planting at St Michael's Mount is inspired and witty. The limited number of plausible plants for such an extreme situation are used in innovative ways and with real panache, providing cameos to admire on the journey but always in tune with the bigger picture.

or tend those already there. It is small wonder that the people who work here refer to their job as "gardening on the edge".

Often in other parts of the garden at St Michael's Mount, where there seems to be earth and a level surface, someone will optimistically dig down to plant an agave or a cordyline, only to find their spade hitting rock just a few centimetres below the soil surface. A lot of seaside gardening is hit-and-miss, but here it is particularly so. But if a big plant needing a decent-sized planting hole is not a viable option, there are many alternative plants that will thrive happily in the space: for example, gazanias or lampranthus need little soil around their roots and make a fine show, as do self-sown plants such as the dramatic *Echium pininana*, a relative of the wild viper's bugloss.

There are several distinct areas on the island, including a woodland on the shady, north-facing side, where camellias and rhododendrons hold sway. There are also walled areas on the flatter part towards the summit, where subtropical gardens and sweeping

Above – Wooden obelisks, formers for topiary, provide structure themselves. In this bed, though edges are straight and surfaces, walls, and paths flat and colour still edited, the planting of mounding subshrubs and perennials, punctuated by the needles of grasses and libertias, gives the whole area a feeling of freshness and innovation.

Opposite – In contrast to the wild, yet still adhering to the maxim of maintaining continuity, the hand of man is here more evident. In order to plant up one of the few flat areas within the garden, full use has been made of symmetry and geometric forms. The materials and many plants are the same as elsewhere, but they are introduced here with control and deliberation.

avenues of a more formal nature than those of the wild slopes provide a sheltered retreat. The first walled gardens here in the eighteenth century made use of the stored heat and the full light to grow stone fruit and soft fruit as well as a multitude of glorious ornamental plants.

The steep terraces are designed to be viewed from above, but you can clamber down paths and steps and get close up and personal with the plants – not too close, though, with some of the yuccas and agaves. There are more than a hundred terraces here, some small, some large. All are designed so they can be planted with exotic species from around the world – St Michael's Mount was a popular venue for the wealth of plants brought into the UK from far-flung locations in the era of discovery and colonial "exploration".

Now that the "rock in the forest" has become a "rock in the sea" there are lessons to be gleaned and inspiration to be had from the majestic gardens at St Michael's Mount. Above all else they remind us that adopting a creative outlook on the plants we can grow and what we can do with them in our seaside setting are all-important.

101

Seaside plant directory

Agave americana 'Variegata'
The leaves of this splendid sculptural plant can grow as big as 1.5m (5ft). They have serrated edges, spiny and fierce, and are striped boldly with cream. This variety is grown for its foliage, but when it does flower, the blooms can be enormous; sadly the plant will die afterwards, because it is monocarpic. It is tender but will succeed in most seaside places.

Phormium 'Jester'
If you want something sharp, architectural but that will stand up to all manner of gales and fierce conditions, then nothing really beats this phormium. The leaves are very fibrous; indeed, in its native New Zealand, phormium is used to make fabrics. With its bronze, coral, and cream foliage, this glamorous plant looks right with everything.

Coronilla valentina
This plant needs a sheltered position unless it is grown in very poor soil and by the sea, in which case it will live for years and years. It is a legume, as can be seen by the typically shaped, pea-like flowers, whose amazing scent can often be detected during winter, as this is a plant that will flower for months on end. Its flowers are brilliant yellow.

Gazania 'Bicton Orange'
Being vibrant and colourful, gazanias have been hybridized hugely in recent years, and an enormous number of cultivars are available. The most striking are those with silvery foliage, which look perfect in a seaside setting. They love dry, sandy soil. Propagate from seed or, in early spring, from short basal cuttings in gritty compost, with bottom heat.

Hippophae rhamnoides
Often seen around coasts and widely distributed in parts of Asia and Europe, sea buckthorn (*Hippophae rhamnoides*) also survives high above the tree line, so is a real toughie. It has slender, silvery leaves and is dioecious, with male and female flowers on separate plants. The pollen is borne by the wind. Female plants usually bear a rich crop of berries.

Eryngium maritimum

This spiky sea holly (*Eryngium maritimum*) is one of the most spectacular plants in its native UK. It lives only in sand dunes and needs a huge depth of sand to thrust down its big taproots. It will withstand gales, salt, and everything else that the climate can throw at it. It is totally tough and even in the far north of the UK will thrive brilliantly well.

Lupinus arboreus

Tree lupins (*Lupinus arboreus*) compete seriously with Jack's fabled beanstalk. Given the right conditions, seeds sown in early spring will produce a plant up to 1.8m (6ft) tall and as much across. It is short-lived, but since new plants are easily raised, this really does not matter. Ideal for filling gaps in a border, it tolerates any amount of sea spray and wind.

Helichrysum italicum

Often known as curry plant because of the strong, resinous scent of its leaves, *Helichrysum italicum* is a subshrub, typical of the kind of plants that grow on Mediterranean shores. It has skinny leaves and dense, bushy growth. Its long-lasting flowers, silver in bud, become bright yellow on opening. It can be used as a dried flower but has quite a pungent aroma.

Crambe maritima

From the first emergence of its tight, purple shoots to the last demise of its skeletal stems and bead-like seed capsules, sea kale (*Crambe maritima*) is a star performer. Essentially it is a cabbage, sharing with the rest of the brassica family two olfactory characteristics: its flowers are sweetly scented, but its leaves are cabbagey (think school dinners!).

Santolina chamaecyparissus 'Edward Bowles'

Cotton lavender (*Santolina chamaecyparissus*) is a familiar subshrub. It needs very little, apart from being grown in full sun. The poorer the soil the better it will perform. This variety has a pleasing texture (its foliage is small, grey, and very dense), especially when covered in pale lemon flowers.

Olearia 'Waikariensis'

Daisy bush (*Olearia*) from New Zealand is a signature shrub of seaside gardens. Insects feast on its pollen and nectar, smothered as it is with white or pale pink daisies all summer long. It has tough, leathery foliage, which enables it to cope brilliantly well with a maritime climate or with any exposed site. It fits perfectly into a seaside picture.

103

Stachys byzantina
This Middle Eastern plant has long been a real favourite in British gardens. It needs sun. It is known in our house as the "ticky" plant, because my daughters adopted it as a comforter when they were little and they would rub their noses with it. It is soft and very furry, giving it its affectionate common names of lambs' lugs or lambs' ears.

Festuca glauca 'Elijah Blue'
Festuca is a very fashionable grass for a hot, dry, sunny place. It makes dwarf mounds, and I think it looks best planted randomly in big swathes with an occasional continuation into other plants as though it had self-seeded. Avoid planting it in lines or as an edging! It is ideal for a container if you want to make a mini Mediterranean garden.

Grevillea 'Olympic Flame'
This plant looks as though it belongs at the seaside. It is an antipodean one with very fine, needle-like leaves and strange, spidery flowers, which in this variety are bright red. It is slightly on the tender side, so, if you are planting grevillea inland, choose a sheltered position. It needs full sun, prefers acid soil, and does not mind gale-force winds!

Armeria maritima
This is the county flower of the Scilly Isles. It is found all through Europe and elsewhere in the northern hemisphere, also in South America. It requires full sun, poor soil, and an exposed position on which to make its dense tussocks of slender leaves, from which extend beautiful, allium-like flowers. They are a lovely texture and look perfect among rocks or in gravel.

Erigeron glaucus
Beach aster (*Erigeron glaucus*) is from the Californian coast, where it grows in sand dunes. Its tough, spoon-shaped leaves are thick and impervious to salt spray. Over them spread a marvellous array of pink daisies. Each of these composite flowers contains lots and lots of tiny blooms, which provide nectar and pollen galore for bees and hoverflies.

Perovskia 'Blue Spire'
Russian sage (*Perovskia*) is a subshrub from central Asia. It is not actually related to sage, but it does have very aromatic foliage and produces tall spires of tiny, purple flowers. It is indomitable, drought-tolerant, and will last through just about anything, provided it has excellent drainage and is planted in full sun. Makes a haze of soft colour.

Lavatera arborea

Lavatera arborea relishes open and exposed positions and can cope with any amount of salt, which it actually excretes through its foliage, because of the way it has evolved. These leaves are round and soft, and the plant is in flower for months on end. It is a native plant found around UK coasts and throughout Europe. Tough, fast, and easy to grow.

Erysimum 'Bowles's Mauve'

This well-known subshrub is very good-natured and tolerant and seldom out of flower. Like other brassicas, it has a big, long taproot, but because of its size and the rapidity of its growth, it is subject to windrock and sometimes needs replacing. This is easy to do by taking little cuttings. It is a very fine plant – one not to be without in any maritime garden.

Rosa 'Roseraie de l'Haÿ'

This is a cultivar of *Rosa rugosa*, a coastal rose from the shores of Japan. It has taken up residence in large parts of the South Wales coastline. In sandy conditions it will sucker around, making quite a thicket. It has big flowers, ravishing and highly scented. In *Rosa rugosa*, these are followed by hips, but even this double-flowered version often produces them.

Lathyrus tingitanus

Tangier pea (*Lathyrus tingitanus*) comes from North Africa but is now widely distributed all over the world, including the Pacific Northwest. It is an annual. Its flowers are produced singly, although there will be many to a plant. It has an exquisite form and a striking colour, varying from pale pink to deep, bright magenta. Easy to grow in a sandy site.

Ruschia

The flowers of this South African plant, closely related to *Lampranthus* and *Mesembryanthemum*, almost cover the plant, so you can barely see the small, succulent leaves at all. Ruschia is diurnal, so its flowers close at night. It also shuts them when rain is due, so acting like a barometer. It can vary from being a ground-covering plant to a shrubby bush.

Lavandula angustifolia 'Munstead'

Lavender never looks better than when placed among gravel or stone. It is also fantastic in pure sand. It is great as a hedge and also looks good just as a mounding plant, randomly planted among other Mediterranean subjects. If you need uniform plants, take cuttings; otherwise they are easy to grow from seed. Its perfume is optimized in hot, dry conditions.

exposed

Although the British Isles are not subject to the extreme weather that pertains in so many other places in the world, nonetheless the conditions can be challenging, especially if you make a living from the land or you are gardening. Relentless winds can flatten everything in sight and even bend and sculpt trees and shrubs – reflecting their force. Soil can be thin, poor, and arid or sometimes marshy, acid, and so low in nutrients that it is surprising anything will grow. But it can – and it does.

- -

Gardening in Exposed Places

Opposite – Our garden is exposed. There are fields, hedges, and woods aplenty between us and the ocean, which is only 16–19km (10–12 miles) away. Nowadays by far the most exposed part of the garden is the green roof we have made on top of the shed. I am always greedy for space and I love the new gardening challenges the roof garden creates. Despite the weight of soil, not to mention mine, the shed is holding up so far. The planting is still at the experimental stage. Should I water or should I see which the survivors are?

SO MANY OF US live in towns and cities, where, even when they are cooler or at a higher altitude than most, the gardens within them have shelter from the elements. In bigger cities, especially, a microclimate affords warmer temperatures. But on the outskirts of those cities and on the moors and mountains that lie beyond them, conditions can be much more challenging.

Those who live on an island – or a series of islands – are particularly at the mercy of the weather, which is ever changing. The British climate is called temperate, but many of us, especially those who garden in exposed places, feel it is anything but that. It is a maritime temperate climate strongly influenced by proximity to the sea, and the fluctuations in temperature are mild in comparison to those of a continental climate. Even mainland Europe, because of its greater landmass, is subject to extremes of temperature, colder winters, and hotter summers, which the British Isles being surrounded by the ocean seldom experience. It is frequently windy in the British Isles, and the higher you are or the closer to the sea the windier it can be. Most of the prevailing winds and most of the weather come from the west – from the Atlantic.

In any garden it is important to choose the right plants, those that will feel at home in the conditions offered. Many plants are

Above – Pinks (Dianthus) *are archetypal cliff-dwellers. Not only can they cope with little or no soil, but they also seem to revel in it; and high alkalinity holds no fear for them – the limier the better. This toughness translates directly to garden varieties.*

Opposite – These two cultivated pinks, Dianthus *'Elizabethan' and* D. *'Glebe Cottage White', delight in crunchy, poor potting compost with masses of grit in a shallow pot. Sun is the major requirement.*

very accommodating and their tolerance levels are high; if they are planted in rather more shade than they are used to, if the soil is a bit wetter than that of their native habitat, most will adapt to cope with these minor changes in conditions.

But to ask the mainstream plants, which make up the backbone of our beds and borders, to survive where the soil is as thin as dust, to persuade them that they can take up residence on a vertical cliff, blasted by gale-force winds or, equally, that a peat bog with zilch nutrients to offer would be an ideal set-up, then those plants would refuse – they would sulk, suffer, and eventually die.

When gardening on an exposed site, there are numerous strategies we can adopt to ameliorate the situation – create shelter, enrich the soil, and remove stones – but in the end there is only one way to guarantee success and that is to put in plants and create communities of those plants that will thrive and flourish. We need to look to mountains and moors, scree, rock, and highland bog, both around us and in similar locations around the world, to discover the plants that will make any exposed garden blossom and burgeon.

111

Plant adaptations

Every plant in the world has evolved to survive in the conditions in which it grows, and all its constituent parts – its flowers, roots, stems, and leaves – play their part in this strategy for survival.

If you are a plant that lives in a hot, dry situation, sometimes subjected to drying winds, your leaves must find ways of retaining moisture, to prevent them becoming desiccated. The moment a leaf is completely unable to function is when that plant will start to die. There are many solutions to this problem and various plants cope in different ways. Some reduce their leaf surface and produce tiny, needle-like leaves – heathers (*Erica*) are a good example.

Others follow the same principle of leaf minimizing but adopt much-divided leaves, often going a step further and coating these skinny, ferny leaves with hairs to make them grey or silver and to reflect as much light and heat as possible. Many wormwoods (*Artemisia*) adopt this practice.

Other plants may produce much larger leaves – often in a rosette – so that any available moisture runs back into the centre of each rosette; but again they are coated with hairs. Many of the plants with *lanata* (meaning "woolly") in their title have such foliage. Lambs' lugs (*Stachys lanata*, now known as *S. byzantina*) is covered in a furry, woolly coating, not only on its leaves but also on its stems and bracted flower spikes. *Salvia argentea* and *S. aethiopis* rely on the same technique, and many verbascums do the same.

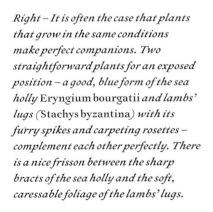

Right – It is often the case that plants that grow in the same conditions make perfect companions. Two straightforward plants for an exposed position – a good, blue form of the sea holly Eryngium bourgatii *and lambs' lugs (*Stachys byzantina*) with its furry spikes and carpeting rosettes – complement each other perfectly. There is a nice frisson between the sharp bracts of the sea holly and the soft, caressable foliage of the lambs' lugs.*

Above left – The very blatant contrast here relies on both colour and texture, the foliage of these two plants being on the same scale. The branching, silvery spikes of santolina are a perfect foil for the crimson carpet created by the stonecrop (Sedum).

Above right – The two greens are a perfect match, while the form and texture of these carpeting plants – woundwort (Stachys) and a needle-leaved euphorbia – create a fascinating pattern.

There are even furry flowers. Pasque flower (*Pulsatilla vulgaris*) is the furriest of all. Its flowers, stems, and petals are covered in down. Before the flowers even think of making an appearance, the finely cut leaves materialize. They are ferny and silvered at first, emerging tentatively like inquisitive sea anemones as if to feel the air. When pasque flower is grown in the poor conditions that suit it best, the silvery sheen is at its most pronounced. It relishes thin, alkaline soils and loves an open, sunny situation. This is the case with all these plants that have evolved in "hostile", exposed environments. If you spoil them by giving them a lush living with fertile loam and by feeding them, they will become quite unlike themselves with soft and soggy leaves and etiolated growth, and in the longer term they will not be able to cope and so will die.

Another clever adaptation is size of leaf. It is not just heathers and gorse (*Ulex*) that have tiny leaves but also many other plants we associate with heath and high exposure. Thyme (*Thymus*) is a good example. The size of its leaf, where little water is lost through

Above left – The leaf shapes of a New Zealand burr (Acaena) *echo the shapes of the chippings through which it grows. The only difference is that the plant moves around whereas the stones remain static.*

Above right – Euphorbia myrsinites *frequents arid mountainsides in the Middle East. Its low, sprawling growth makes it the perfect candidate for a similar situation in the garden while the small chippings add to the textural effect.*

transpiration, as well as the stature of the plant – ground hugging – acts as a defence against battering winds.

Some leaves actually move in response to wind and lack of moisture. For example, many grasses can roll up their leaves to reduce leaf surface and retain moisture.

If you are an evergreen and live in a windy place, then you must have tough, thick leaves to prevent your foliage from shrivelling. *Elaeagnus × ebbingei* is often recommended for seaside or hillside planting. It has tough, leathery leaves and their reverse is silvery white, coated with fur to stop evaporation. Conifers have skinny leaves or needles (the clue is in the name) and both junipers (*Juniperus*) – native to some heathland – and pines (*Pinus*) have successfully evolved, surviving not only blasting winds and frequent droughts but ice ages too. Their tough, resinous, scaly bark also helps. Trees are seldom a feature of moorland but the rowan (*Sorbus aucuparia*) and the birch (*Betula*) are past masters at survival on mountain tops and in thin, acid soils.

*Right – The wiry, steel-wool effect
of the santolina, with its twiggy,
upward-facing stems, crowns the top
of the wall and is perfectly at home.
Cascading down the wall, in front,
lampranthus drinks in the sunshine,
its daisy flowers opening wide and
its mat of succulent leaves conserving
water in case of dry times ahead.*

*Opposite – There are cracks and crevices
– both natural and man-made – in
all sorts of structures and, wherever
there is room, there will be a plant
ready to take up residence – in fact,
quite frequently, several plants. Some
of Jonathan Buckley's pictures were
taken on the Burren, in County Clare,
Ireland, where deep creeks and fissures
between rocks support whole gardens.
Clockwise from top left are* Phyteuma
orbiculare, *rock samphire (*Crithmum
maritimum*), bloody cranesbill
(*Geranium sanguineum*), ivy-leaved
toadflax (*Cymbalaria muralis*),
common polypody (*Polypodium
vulgare*), and rusty-back fern
(*Asplenium ceterach*).*

*Overleaf – Naturalized cyclamen and
little blue bulbs create fascinating
patches of pattern and texture among
the mossy stones on the steep slope
of John Massey's perfectly conceived
rock garden.*

Plants for cracks & crevices

In the garden here at Glebe Cottage, where there are few
opportunities to grow plants that need excellent drainage, we
think ourselves lucky that we have a few cracks and crevices in
our dry-stone walls. Because the garden is on a slope we made
broad terraces on the west side of the track and retained them
with dry-stone walls constructed from local building stone –
some salvaged from the garden but more bought locally.

Building dry-stone walls is a hugely rewarding if somewhat
arduous business. And the joy of finding and fitting the right piece
is only half of it. Planting walls with alpines and rock garden plants
is very satisfying, especially when you know they will enjoy the
conditions that fit them to a tee. When you are building a retaining
wall, with soil behind it that you have firmed in from the base
upwards as you build each course, you can be confident that plant
roots will be in intimate contact with the soil behind. What you do
not want to do is push plants in willy-nilly with great air gaps behind
them – those plants can derive neither water nor sustenance from
the soil because they are not touching it. One way round this when
you are building a wall is to plant as you go, ensuring every plant has
the best possible chance of survival. Good planting and a choice of
plants based on emulating nature will pay dividends.

Above left, centre, and right – Most alpines are diminutive and when in bloom have immense "flower power". Presumably this is a policy to draw in pollinating insects at the crucial time. Since their flowers can be neither big nor on tall stems because of the prevailing conditions, alpines have developed strategies for attracting insects using mass flowering and bee-attractive colouring. Here (above left) blue-eyed grass (Sisyrinchium graminoides) from the New World makes a big impact for a little plant. Tulipa clusiana opens its petals wide to draw in visitors (above centre), while a saxifrage typically flourishes in its rocky habitat (above right).

Alpines

Alpines are some of the most misunderstood plants and yet those who are addicted to them are completely hooked. I am one of them.

There has always been discussion among alpine enthusiasts about what constitutes an alpine, purists insisting that alpines were exclusively plants that grew above the tree line, but the Alpine Garden Society has taken a much more liberal approach in recent years. For our purposes, alpines are plants that come from mountain areas and have evolved to cope with the often harsh conditions there. As well as being immensely useful, they are also incredibly beautiful. A few are notoriously difficult to grow but there are thousands that are straightforward and these are exactly the plants we need when our gardens are laid open to the elements. For once we have the advantage over those with safe and sheltered gardens – these plants prefer our places and we can grow them more successfully.

Alpines are magical. There is a dramatic contrast between these tiny, jewel-like plants and the awe-inspiring places they grow. It is probably that juxtaposition that attracts people to rock gardens and the plants themselves. There is something about the "call of the mountains" that makes it such an attractive proposition to emulate. Realistically for many people with small plots or those who do not even have a garden, the best way to re-create this sort of feeling and to introduce these sorts of plants is to use a trough or a big bowl and

Above left – Polygala calcaria *'Lillet'*
is a pretty milkwort that relishes an
alkaline soil.

Above centre – Ranunculus alpestris
is a tough but very pretty, little plant
whose simple flowers open wide to
the sun and are loaded with pollen
and nectar.

Above right – *Many cyclamen such*
as this C. coum *are at home in*
harsh conditions.

create a mini rock garden. Providing there is adequate drainage,
soil-based compost incorporating plenty of grit, a few rocks (tufa is
the best because it is as light as a feather but looks the part) and there
is a good selection of suitable plants, you can conjure at least a breath
of mountain air with your alpine display.

Where there are rocks or stone in the garden or walls and features
built of stone, there are endless possibilities for crevice alpines –
the plants that insinuate themselves between rocky fissures in the
mountains. The saxifrage family is enormous and several divisions
of it are ideal to grow in these conditions. The close-knit Kabschia
saxifrages (*Saxifraga*) flower early in the year and are sometimes
studded so prolifically with flowers that the foliage is invisible.
Many of the encrusted saxifrages, which, as their name suggests,
are covered with a protective layer, giving their leaves a tough, hard
surface, make rosette after rosette, thereby filling crannies quietly
until, in spring, their extraordinary flower stems shoot upwards
decorated with sprays of tiny flowers.

Many alpines love to live "on the vertical". The popular *Primula
auricula* – so often grown in pots or as a border plant – is happiest
when growing on its side, so that water drains away from its fleshy
roots. Like saxifrages and so many of these crevice-dwellers, its
roots can penetrate the rock, extracting water and nutrients and
maintaining itself in what can be a very precarious position.

Exposed maritime

Even though a whole chapter of this book concentrates on gardening by the sea, it would be unforgivable in a chapter that is specifically about exposed sites not to mention the problems encountered for those who garden by the sea and have to cope with stony, gravelly soil or pure sand and relentless, buffeting winds.

There are few trees that will survive such inhospitable situations, yet nature abhors a vacuum and there are some, as well as a few shrubs, that have manoeuvred themselves into the vacant slots. The olive (*Olea*) tree pictured above, though it may not be *au fait* with the saline conditions, is certainly well acquainted with droughty conditions and poor soil and fits itself admirably into the vacancy. Its small leaves are almost impervious to lack of moisture and it is used to going without for a long time.

Sea purslane or salt-plant (*Atriplex halimus*) has similar qualities. It is a vastly underrated shrub, looking well turned out at all times, with its branches covered in glistening silver leaves. As its common names suggest, it is happy at the seaside but it also makes an ideal windbreak or just a feature plant in any garden exposed to wind and

Above – A knobbly, old olive looks perfectly at home in this seaside garden, overlooking the other action that is taking place around it. Low shrubs, juniper (Juniperus), and broom (Genista) wend their way backwards and forwards, while mats of thyme (Thymus) at a lower level make a still closer carpet. Here and there the vivid magenta flowers of dusty miller (Lychnis coronaria) emblazon the scene.

Above – The delights of self-seeding plants are the surprises that they produce. Some of the best ideas I have ever had are copied from the combinations and associations between self-seeded plants. Here, poppies (Papaver), *campion* (Lychnis), *and* Galactites tomentosa *share the pitch, while the silvery clumps of leymus – our most successful seaside grass – assert themselves here and there.*

stormy weather. Cuttings are easy to root. Leaves are edible too, as sea purslane is related to spinach – and they come ready-salted.

The gravel and sand of many seaside scenarios are ideal ground in which seeds can germinate. Colonies of successful plants can make happy and naturalistic schemes.

Often short-lived perennials and biennials will populate an area of seaside garden. Sometimes our own plantings lack the artless charm of these spontaneous creations but often our own deliberate plantings can be enhanced by them. One of the loveliest sights is when these "gate crashers" come up through the middle and around the perimeters of low-carpeting and scrambling plants. Spaces can be left or cleared for paths to meander through such a seaside wonderland, and it is nice to have to step around plants – it makes the journey along the path less of a route and more of an interesting adventure. Such schemes work best both aesthetically and practically if they are mulched in gravel, shingle, or pebbles, preferably to tally with whatever material predominates naturally. Such a mulch also provides excellent drainage, making the plants better prepared for the challenging conditions.

Containers

Although as gardeners we use containers for all sorts of plants, they lend themselves particularly to subjects that come from the high hills and mountains.

For a container, the rules are even more stringent than the normal ones of planting anywhere. Provide the plant with what it needs, put it in a situation where it would choose to live, and give it regular maintenance. It must have the last because in a garden context a plant is presented with no options – it has to live as and where it is told – whereas in the wild it would fit in with its situation.

Unless you are growing some of the few shade-loving alpines, such as haberleas or hepaticas, pots, troughs, and containers need to be placed in a sunny, exposed place and require well-drained, loam-based potting compost with masses of extra grit. An advantage of growing alpines in pots is that you can tailor their compost to their needs and possibly grow plants that might find it difficult to survive in your garden soil.

Containers are as varied as the plants you can grow in them. It is not for me to pronounce on aesthetics but pots and containers are always secondary – they are a means to grow plants and as such they should never compete with the plants, but always enhance them. Natural materials, clay, stone, metal are always preferable to plastic. I always wonder what it must be like for a plant to live in a plastic pot. Any container is unremitting but at least clay breathes and is porous.

Opposite above – The joy of creating one vast splurge, celebrating one joyous moment in the year's calendar, is entirely possible when you plant in a container. Here Cyclamen coum *forms a carpet, its vivid, reflexed flowers mixing perfectly with the round, silvered leaves through which grow snowdrops (*Galanthus*), making a little canopy.*

*Opposite below – The succulent rosettes of houseleek (*Sempervivum*) are a stark contrast to the sharp, geometric texture of their containers.*

Below left and centre – The simplicity of houseleek in a piece of broken terracotta, or a hepatica in its Japanese pot, could not be bettered.

Below right – Alpines in containers can be very simple or you can turn them into a mini landscape with dwarf conifers and rocks. If they are underplanted with bulbs in a trough or sink, you can extend the flowering season through spring, summer, and into autumn.

Green roofs

Space is so often at a premium in modern gardens that it is important to capitalize on every square metre. Whether it is a shed or a bike shelter, the top of any structure can be turned into a home for plants. With good planning and the right plants, a green roof can establish itself as a viable community that needs little intervention. As concrete jungles continue to expand, green roofs can help to redress the ecological balance – a tiny step, but in the right direction. Thus they can be an oasis for wildlife and a huge pleasure for us to enjoy. Such places, however, require careful planting, as they are very exposed to all types of weather.

Building a green roof is experimental to say the least – every roof is different and there are no templates to follow. When we had to move our nursery at Glebe Cottage, and our potting shed along with it, we used the opportunity to create a green roof.

Neil, my husband, reinforced, raised, and reversed the pitch of the roof so we could see it from higher up the garden. The next step was to cover the corrugated steel with underfelt and pond liner.

Above – You might think there is quite enough garden at Glebe Cottage already without going up in the world and planting a roof, but like so many other people I feel that everything should be done to maximize a garden's usefulness to wildlife. A couple of years ago we seized the opportunity to elevate our planting here to a whole new level.

Opposite above – Many flat roofs lend themselves to conversion to a green roof. Weight, stress, and drainage are important factors to consider before undertaking such a project.

Opposite below – Wild carrot (Daucus carota) does well on a roof, but its stature and vigour will be determined by the depth of soil. In shallow soil it will be less significant.

We used a honeycombed soil retainer and, as we planted, filled it with topsoil from our old nursery beds and with sterilized loam. I wanted to grow a wide range of plants to offer food and shelter to as many insects as possible over a long period.

Another (easier) alternative would have been to make a stonecrop (*Sedum*) roof. You can even buy such things by the square metre; once it is unrolled, it will come back to life. Biting stonecrop (*S. acre*), the UK's most common stonecrop, is one of the main constituents of most proprietary, green roof products. We are all familiar with its bright yellow stars and its plump, ovoid leaves which, when they break off, root readily even without any proper soil. These leaves taste peppery. English stonecrop (*S. anglicum*) and white stonecrop (*S. album*) are also part of most roofing mixes. If a plant will grow on a roof, it must be pretty tough. Each of their leaves needs to be fat and fleshy, plump with water reserves that can keep it going almost indefinitely. Even when conditions are really dry, plants decimated by drought will make a rapid comeback as soon as water is made available to them.

127

At first sight, areas of Wildside might look as bleak as the landscape of Dartmoor, UK, which surrounds the garden, but even where earthworks are still under way, they will not remain so for long as Keith Wiley wields his wizard's wand. Soon they will be populated with some of the most special plants you could imagine.

Case study 6

Making the Most of the Moorland

Above – For many years Keith's most important gardening tool was his mechanical digger. With it he turned a flat site into a fascinating landscape, tripling the planting area in many parts of the garden. Yet however he manipulates the land, it is the plants he grows there and the way they are put together that is at the heart of the garden.

Opposite – In the soft West Country light this monolith, surrounded by perovskia and lilting grasses, looks as if it could have been standing here for aeons.

Overleaf – The garden at Wildside is a masterpiece not only of colour and form but of texture too.

KEITH AND ROS WILEY'S relatively new garden, Wildside, already has a glowing reputation among gardeners. Set close to Buckland Monachorum near Dartmoor, UK, it is a living example of how to succeed on an exposed site.

To call Wildside awe-inspiring is to understate the effect it has on you. Walk in there on a sun-kissed afternoon in mid-summer and you will be transported to another place. You will forget about everything else. Everywhere you look, your eye will alight on treasures, stands of angel's fishing rods (*Dierama*), lilting grasses, and African blue lilies (*Agapanthus*) like you have never seen them before, melded into a molten mass that flows up and down the gentle slopes and either side of your wending route. In this garden, plants rule because they are given what they need and love and they are allowed to be themselves.

Keith knows his plants intimately and grows them to perfection. He has seen many of them in their native habitats and studied the ways in which they develop as individuals and vis-à-vis their neighbours. His planting is informed by an intimate knowledge of plant communities and applying it to his own gardening efforts.

Keith is a visionary. His ideas are original and it is impossible to tag him. He must present a challenge to those who feel it is

Right – In contrast to the striking structure and vibrant colour of the red hot pokers, in places at Wildside there are almost monochromatic plantings with detailed texture, such as the dark stems of Sedum telephium *'Purple Emperor' alongside* Dierama dracomontanum.

Opposite above left – It is easy to see why Kniphofia *has earned the handle of red hot poker. This member of the lily family comes from heathland and grassland on mountain slopes, often in damp soil, in southern and eastern Africa. Therefore the assumption in the common name is that plants that come from "hot" countries must like dry conditions.*

Opposite above right – One of the daisy bushes, Olearia × haastii, *makes wonderful, lumpy mounds. Flourishing in poor soil, it is usually hardy and needs little attention. It is just perfect with these soft stipa.*

Opposite below left and right – Sometimes the contrasts at Wildside are bold and blatant, while at other times there are subtle associations. There is as much of a place for the lemon bobbles of santolina (below far left) as for the orange spikes of Castilleja miniata *(below left), flaming their way upwards through soft lavender (*Lavandula*). Everything belongs.*

imperative to categorize. His inspiration is nature, and though he never tries to copy it – an absurd aim – he emulates it at every opportunity. Whether it is the wild landscape that surrounds the garden or the communities of plants he has witnessed first hand on the South African veld, his planting abounds with echoes of nature.

Nowhere do you feel that Keith is influenced by horticultural history, nor by present trends. There is none of the kowtowing to The Emperor and his new clothes that permeates so much of current garden design. He has always been too interested in the places he has visited, the plants he has seen and, more than anything, his vision for his own garden to notice, yet alone follow, the dictates of fashion.

For the landscape of Wildside, Keith wanted to create habitats and situations for different sorts of plants. Some of the slopes of his earthworks are south-facing and in full light – sometimes even in full sun all day. That means that the corresponding slope on the other side of these man-made mountains is in shade. There are chances to grow a wide array of shade-lovers, sun-worshippers, and everything in between. Eventually there will be wetland areas too – ponds and streams and all the plants that go with them.

But Wildside is 180m (600ft) above sea level and is subjected to buffeting winds, sporadic snow, and occasionally gales from the Atlantic. These are the overriding conditions that inform how Keith gardens here, and it is his success in coping with them that makes these few hectares such a source of inspiration to those of us who garden in similar circumstances but on a much smaller scale.

*Opposite – As the hillside is foreshortened, plants undulate, receding into the distance. The late sun backlights the scene, silhouetting each flower of every spike of the enormous clumps of penstemon and catmint (*Nepeta*) and highlighting the soft and fluffy inflorescences of the grasses interspersed between perennials.*

Below – Many of the plants in this area make rounded clumps – what you might call "tumps" if you came from Wales. Each clump of anthemis and santolina has room to nestle down and coexist peacefully with its neighbours.

Overleaf – Some gardeners find Dierama pulcherrimum *difficult to grow. At Wildside it produces magnificent clumps.*

In terms of removing soil when accommodating plants that love poverty and, in juxtaposition, endowing those that love a richer living, Keith has gone several steps further than any of us would be willing or able to. The overriding lesson, though, is not a consequence of his earth-moving nor his ambitious plans. It is just the recognition that in an exposed site like Wildside we can all create beauty by going along with the conditions, choosing plants that love to live there, and giving them the opportunity to do whatever it is that they do as naturally and straightforwardly as possible.

We may elect to use indigenous species or plants that come from other parts of the world or a mixture of both, but if we select them because we know they will cope with harsh, exposed conditions and we can give them what they need in terms of soil, drainage, and light, then our gardens will be happy places. It is the spirit of the place and the plants within it that make a garden. Rather than slavishly following a set of rules, if we recognize the opportunities that exposed sites can offer, we can create a magical garden full of life and energy, as at Wildside.

Moorgate Crofts Business Centre is a state-of-the-art, environmentally friendly building providing managed small office business units. Its roof offers succour to those who work there and is a paradise for pollinating insects – a welcome resource in the midst of post-industrial Rotherham, UK. The planting in the garden quietly echoes the distant moors.
- - - - - - - - - - - - - - - - - - - -

Case study 7
- - - - - - - - - - - - - - - - - -

A Haven for Pollinators & People

Above – Weight and depth of soil are important considerations when planting on a roof. A community of plants needs to be established that will survive happily with little soil and water and no extra nutrients. These plants have no access to subsoil or even rock, and those that survive most successfully are used to hardship in their native habitats.

*Opposite – Being set against the glass and steel of a typical modern building, lambs' lugs (*Stachys byzantina*), wild marjoram (*Origanum vulgare*), lady's bedstraw (*Galium verum*), and native grasses make a thought-provoking contrast. How wonderful that buildings whose footprints obliterated flora are now being used as a place to reassert the flora. How tough and robust these plants are. They will survive long after buildings have crumbled.*

WE ARE INCREASINGLY aware of what useful and beautiful places the roofs of the buildings we live and work in can become. Nigel Dunnett's roof garden overlooking the industrial landscape of Rotherham, Yorkshire, UK, is a good example.

Nigel's garden on the roof of the city's Moorgate Crofts Business Centre represents the current trend for green roofs, which are not only sustainable and wildlife-friendly, but also collect and manage rainwater, and provide insulation for many new and, occasionally, older buildings. Such places have become eco mainstream and have even developed their own academic specialism! Nigel's full title is Reader in Urban Horticulture, Department of Landscape, University of Sheffield or Professor of Planting Design and Vegetation Technology. The new-found respectability for green roofs has helped it tick boxes and become integrated into the contemporary architectural design process. This is all to the good, of course, as local authorities and councils, as well as individuals, embrace its ideas.

Using plants that will tolerate drought and neglect and need little or no maintenance are two of the prime tenets of these green roofs. In their wild incarnations, such plants inhabit mountain slopes, arid plains, and steep cliffs. Their requirements for water and nutrients

Above and opposite – To enjoy this roof garden at Moorgate Crofts, you have to forget all your expectations that a garden should be full, lush, and bursting with flowers. Instead, you need to recognize the fight for survival taking place here and enjoy the colonies of plants that survive, as well as applaud the audacious splashes of colour from Lavandula latifolia *(above left), lambs' lugs (*Stachys byzantina*) (above right), red hot poker (*Kniphofia*) (opposite left), and erodium (opposite right).*

are modest, while their tolerance of wind, sun, and even snow is remarkable. Frequently they are colonizers, whose roots knit together into shallow mats. They often grow low, making close-knit carpets. Most self-seed or have spreading roots and stoloniferous growth, sending out runners that root as they develop.

Green roofs slow rainwater run-off, absorb carbon dioxide, and provide habitats, particularly for invertebrates. Where there is access for human beings, they are also places where people can relax and enjoy a sojourn closer to nature.

Climatic conditions, building styles, and local availability of suitable materials in some countries, especially in isolated rural areas, mean that making green roofs is an established practice. For the rural communities where green roofs are a tradition, their prime purposes are shelter and insulation. In Finland and Norway, for example, roofs lined with birch bark are traditionally overlaid with turf sods. They become a haven for wild flowers and grasses and the creatures that depend on them.

Overleaf – The Mediterranean comes to Rotherham. The maquis planting contrasts with the urbanscape beyond.

Such methods are time-tested in Scandinavia, but would be inappropriate in inner-city Rotherham, where the materials are unavailable locally and would not work when overlaying vastly different structures and materials or in such a different and much drier environment. In principle it is a good idea to have any garden on a roof – though some are more sustainable than others. Roof gardens as a separate concept from green roofs can be extravagant in terms of materials, time, and other resources. Some are merely stage sets for conspicuous consumption and, as such, contribute little to the local ecology or community. On the other hand, if plants are carefully chosen and grown sensibly and sustainably, roof gardens can be a huge asset to the environment.

One of the most important tools we have at our disposal when creating gardens in these inhospitable places is our ability to observe. Without any particular horticultural expertise, but just by careful studying, we can understand how these plants cope with the situations we can offer them.

141

Above left, centre, and right – It is reassuring to see these plants being themselves within the clearly allotted steel and concrete sections of their built and clearly defined confines – but are they confines? Plants self-seed into cracks between pavings, and some just ignore all barriers. Try telling Cypress spurge (Euphorbia cyparissias) (above centre) to stay where you have decided it should grow.

Opposite – The roof garden provides a haven for high-flying insects. There is plenty of nectar and pollen up here.

Plants seldom grow as individuals, so it is important to understand the ways in which they develop together, in association with one another. We may not necessarily use those self-same plants; we can ring the changes, vary the mix, and include different plants that grow in the same conditions.

If the scramble and general free-for-all of some "naturalistic schemes" does not appeal, something more formal can be achieved, though these sorts of plants generally look best when allowed to be themselves. One lovely idea is to use a single species or selection in big chunks, perhaps to fit within a preordained space. Very often in the wild, multiple examples of one plant will spread themselves over a considerable area. You have only to think of heather moors or a carpet of thyme (*Thymus*) to be reminded of how even small plants such as these can have a big impact.

Sometimes a slightly taller plant – perhaps with a more elegant physique – may appear here and there. You could plant bulbs, species crocus, or tulips (*Tulipa*) that reach only a few centimetres high, to grow through such carpets and provide a crescendo of colour in the spring.

You can intervene or leave alone but whatever you do – however hard it may seem at times – you can be sure that the plants of moor and mountain will lend enchantment to your planting on an exposed rooftop.

144

Exposed plant directory

Artemisia ludoviciana '**Valerie Finnis**'

The wormwoods (*Artemisia*) in general enjoy an exposed site. They are extremely tough and all have silvery leaves, developed to withstand drought, windy weather, and full sun. If you need to control them, get your shears and cut them right back to the base. Within weeks they will have refreshed themselves.

Cistus × *cyprius*

Most rock roses (*Cistus*) have sticky leaves covered with a sort of gum, which protects the cuticle of the leaf from harsh sun and high winds. *Cistus* × *cyprius* is totally hardy. It has green, aromatic, sticky leaves and splendiferous, tissue-paper flowers in white, with their maroon markings in the centre; these are probably guides to bring in the bees and insects.

Euphorbia myrsinites

Being from the Middle East, where it grows on arid mountainsides, this spurge (*Euphorbia*) loves dry, sunny locations and is especially at home where it can flop over a dry-stone wall or the like. Its close-packed, slightly pointed, glaucous leaves spiral thickly around its dangling stems. In flower by mid-spring, the greenish yellow bracts often turn orange.

Saxifraga '**Tumbling Waters**'

This is one of the most spectacular alpines you could possibly grow, with its rosettes of linear leaves, beautifully symmetrical and encrusted in silver and white, usually the result of lime that the plant absorbs and then extrudes. Its enormous arching stems bear scores of flowers. When it has flowered, though, it dies, being monocarpic.

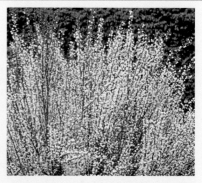

Cytisus × *praecox* '**Albus**'

The whole broom (*Cytisus*) family is good in exposed positions, and this one (*praecox* means "early") makes these great, elegant stems full of white flowers from late spring into early summer. From a distance, it looks just like a white shower. All brooms prefer acid soils and will thrive even when the soil is low in nutrients and thin and well drained.

Lithodora diffusa 'Heavenly Blue'
This plant is actually a member of
the borage family and as such is
very attractive to bees and other
insects. Unlike most borages
(*Borago*), 'Heavenly Blue' prefers
acid conditions. It is great in a gravel
or big rock garden, where it makes a
sizeable clump of spreading stems.
At the end of each stem is borne a
brilliant blue bell, mainly in summer.

Gentiana 'Strathmore'
Many of the plants that are suitable
for an exposed site are spring
flowerers, so it is great to have one
that is at its best later on. Nothing
could beat this gentian's (*Gentiana*)
array of pale azure-blue flowers,
which mingle brilliantly with autumn
leaves. It tolerates a bit of shade,
forms big, trailing stems, and is very
easy to propagate by division.

Hepatica nobilis var. pubescens
This is a European hepatica and
the best one to grow in an exposed,
partially shady site. It does not mind
alkaline soils and generally puts
up with very high exposures. The
flowers are so incredibly pretty that
they look as if they need some special
cosseting and care, but they do not –
they are incredibly hardy. The leaves
are another fine feature.

Nepeta racemosa 'Walker's Low'
As shown, catmints (*Nepeta*) go
beautifully with other plants. They
are unassuming when they mix and
mingle, yet at the same time they
have quite a strong character of their
own. They are extremely tolerant and
put up with neglect, not to mention
having cats roll over them. If chopped
back when the first flowers begin to
fall, they will rebloom in weeks.

Campanula portenschlagiana
The huge bellflower family includes
a vast array of plants from mountain
sites and exposed places, among them
our native harebell (*Campanula
rotundifolia*), which is just a whisper
of a plant. Dalmatian bellflower
(*C. portenschlagiana*) is great in a
dry-stone wall or creeping between
stones. It needs full sun and a hot, dry
site. The soil pH does not matter.

Chionochloa flavescens
I have only recently met this
tussock grass from mountains in
New Zealand. It is a lovely thing
when forming its soft hummocks and
also when its inflorescences appear.
These are soft and close together but
become more feathery through the
season. *Chionochloa flavescens* adores
growing in a hot, dry, sunny place
with great drainage.

Anthemis tinctoria

Nothing could be brighter, more cheerful, or easier than anthemis, which thrives in any open, sunny position. Most are yellow – at times blatant and obvious, as in golden marguerite (*Anthemis tinctoria*) – but *A. t.* 'Sauce Hollandaise' has very pale flowers. Deadheading will bring more blooms, yet flowering will continue all summer in any case.

Coreopsis verticillata 'Moonbeam'

'Moonbeam' is probably my favourite tickseed (*Coreopsis*). It is easy to use and looks so lovely. Like many Central American plants it does not come through until really quite late. I have been known to throw pots of it away and then find it on the compost heap later. So do not be impatient because, once it is in flower, it will go on and on right through to autumn.

Helianthemum nummularium

Many of us will have seen our native rock rose (*Helianthemum*) on dry cliffs and downs. It lies almost flat on the ground, forming large mats, but its great glory is its papery flowers, which are quite big for the size of the plant, and very visible. Hybrids and cultivars of rock roses are available in myriad colours, and they fit very well into a gravel or rock garden.

Dianthus 'Pink Jewel'

Like so many of these alpine pinks (*Dianthus*), this neat, little plant is very small of stature. In fact, it grows to only about 5cm (2in) tall, and it makes tight clumps, bejewelled with highly scented, double flowers. 'Pink Jewel' is perfect not only for a trough or pot, but it also looks lovely in a rock garden growing between rocks.

Stipa tenuissima

This grass has a gorgeous, soft feel and will fit in absolutely anywhere with anything. It is actually an evergreen so never cut it down. There is nothing worse than a stipa with a bad haircut. Just tease or pull out the old, dried stems at the end of winter, and new growth will come through in a matter of weeks. Although short-lived, it does seed around all over the place.

Alyssum oxycarpum

Being a dinky, grey-leaved subshrub that comes from the Turkish mountains, this alyssum is a real alpine and is far removed from the white and pink bedding plants. Each of its little shoots bears a cluster of bright yellow flowers, making the leaves almost invisible when it is in full flower. Grow it in gravel or the crevices between rocks.

Aethionema **'Warley Rose'**
This is a dear, little plant. It is in effect a tiny, pinky purple wallflower, and, like so many of these early flowers, it is smothered in blooms from mid-spring until early summer. 'Warley Rose' will put up with wind and tempest but it needs full sun and poor soil to thrive and so flower beautifully.

Verbascum **'Helen Johnson'**
Hybrid mulleins are exciting. All have big rosettes of felted leaves from which rise tall, straight stems with beautiful flowers, always facing outwards. The buds, contained within their felted overcoats, are lovely too. I adore the terracotta colour of 'Helen Johnson'. It gives such a good vertical accent among mounding grasses and low carpeters.

Pulsatilla vulgaris
The blooms of pasque flower (*Pulsatilla vulgaris*) are quiet and hardly noticeable in dull weather, with their bent heads. However, when the sun shines, the flowers turn their faces towards it – so many stars of rich, deep purple, each lit by a boss of golden stamens with a tufted, purple stigma at its heart. The seedheads complete the furry, fluffy cycle.

Saxifraga 'Dawn Frost'
Kabschia saxifrages, such as 'Dawn Frost', make tight cushions that are almost impervious to moisture. When you touch them, they feel really crunchy, textured, and quite rough. In early spring 'Dawn Frost' is smothered in flowers, but, even when the flowers have fallen, these tight, silvery clumps make a real feature.

Erica carnea **'Springwood Pink'**
In the depths of winter, heathers (*Erica*), especially cultivars of *E. carnea*, come into their own. This species is one of the few heathers that will grow in alkaline soils; it is extremely accommodating and thrives on any site in full light where the soil is not too heavy. 'Springwood Pink' flowers profusely and reliably and is one of the first to show.

Kniphofia
Red hot pokers (*Kniphofia*) are great plants for an exposed site. Many of them come from South Africa, growing high up in the mountains in damp soils. They are members of the lily family, so if you are moving them and splitting them up, do not cut their roots; just pull them apart and plant the rosettes separately. Establish in pots before planting out.

hedgerow

Of all the habitats this book looks at, it is hedgerows that are the most influenced by humankind. They are a man-made phenomenon – some of them are the remnants of ancient woodlands, while most have been planted over the centuries – and have always been used as boundaries. Despite their history, they are one of our richest environments as far as the native flora and fauna they support. They offer inspiration to all gardeners about how to make the best and most beautiful use of their own hedges and edges.

Verdant Boundaries

Opposite – We planted our native hedge many years ago. Every couple of years it is relaid and ends up just 1m (3ft) or so high but thicker each time. Its growth is phenomenal. We leave a few shrubs and trees uncut, including this guelder rose (Viburnum opulus). The dogs give it their full attention.

HEDGES ARE NOT A NATURAL phenomenon – they are man-made. However, along with such plants as wood spurge (*Euphorbia amygdaloides*) and primroses (*Primula vulgaris*), the trees that make up hedgerows – beech (*Fagus*), oak (*Quercus*), ash (*Fraxinus*), and hazel (*Corylus*) – have successfully made the transition from their natural habitat of woodland and woodland edge.

The life of a hedgerow is complex and fascinating. Therefore, the more varied we can make the hedges in our gardens , the richer they will be both in terms of the wildlife they attract and support and the range of plants we can include. As mentioned earlier in this book, the idea is not to copy nature but rather to emulate it and to use wild hedgerows as the inspiration for our garden edges and hedges.

Hedgerows are completely unlike other habitats in several respects. They comprise a unique combination of woody plants – trees and shrubs – alongside grasses, ferns, and flowering plants, with the added attraction of bulbs such as snowdrops (*Galanthus*), daffodils (*Narcissus*), and ornamental onions (*Allium*), including wild garlic (*A. ursinum*) and even, occasionally, chives (*A. schoenoprasum*). Plants that survive in hedgerows have to be especially adaptable. They need to be able to cope with light levels

Above – Growing plants vertically affords so many opportunities for exciting partnerships. The weighty racemes of Chinese wisteria (Wisteria sinensis) *mingle here with the magnificent sepals of* Clematis *'Marie Boisselot'. But this is a* ménage à trois – *on the wall behind* Actinidia kolomitka *bides its time.*

Opposite – Nature has a knack of putting plants together perfectly. That is what evolution is all about. Here the "old man's beards" of Clematis viticella *mingle with a rich autumn crop of hawthorn* (Crataegus) *berries. The hawthorn is a match for the often-strangling growth of the clematis.*

that can change rapidly each day, and also tolerate torrential rain and drought conditions – both light levels and water levels within a hedgerow community can fluctuate wildly.

When we then look at the boundaries of our gardens – even when we do not demarcate them all with hedges – we notice that they have much in common with hedgerows. A bed bordering a wall or fence that runs north to south will spend part of the day in full light and part of it in shadow. If prevailing weather is from the west, as it most certainly is here at Glebe Cottage, then one side of the hedge will receive a lot more water than the other.

Thus hedgerows provide a good indication of plants that will not only survive but also fill the edges of our gardens with colour and verdancy. Though we think of these areas as the edges, they have primary importance, as they occupy a huge area. The smaller the garden, the more important they become. On top of being prime planting areas in their own right, hedges often offer the only opportunity for vertical gardening – growing climbers – for their own beauty and interest and as a backdrop for other plantings.

Beautiful banks

At Glebe Cottage there are several places at the foot of stretches of trees or hedges where the ground rises above the level of the rest of the garden. Though banks like these are not a feature of every garden, it is worth looking at the plants that grow successfully there for similar if not directly analogous places in your own garden – perhaps ones that are steep or awkward.

Plants that live here must have certain characteristics and capabilities. They need to cling on and colonize, first establishing themselves and then spreading out, so that the soil in which they are growing is not eroded and washed away. Low plants with fibrous roots are ideal in such situations. Primroses (*Primula vulgaris*), for example, are naturally bank-dwellers. If you are planting them on a slope, start towards the top. In the wild you always find that they move downwards as seed is self-sown. Periwinkles (*Vinca*) are excellent for such situations too. Their spreading growth is spangled with blue or, occasionally, claret or white flowers early in the year. They root as they grow, a habit shared with bugle (*Ajuga reptans*).

Above – Cyclamen hederifolium *makes itself at home. From the number of its flowers, there must be a giant corm here of a great age – proof positive that this is the perfect environment for this plant to flourish.*

Opposite – *Despite getting hammered in recent years, this hedgerow is flourishing. In early summer, ferns, campion (*Lynchis*), and stitchwort (*Stellaria*) scramble up and down the bank, while climbers – brambles (*Rubus fruticosus*), honeysuckle (*Lonicera*), and dog roses (*Rosa canina*) – are just beginning to rev up for their summer show.*

Overleaf – *The shade at the base of this wall is the perfect venue for* Corydalis flexuosa *and ferns.*

*Above left and right – Although honeysuckle is most fragrant as dusk descends, even during the day, when you grab a sniff, its perfume penetrates not only your nostrils but your very soul too. Our dogs are so used to having their walks punctuated by honeysuckle sniffing – here of common honeysuckle (*Lonicera periclymenum*) – that they almost anticipate each one.*

Opposite – Although honeysuckle is essentially a woodlander, it will latch onto any structure that is offered – be it tree, bank, fence, or wall. With its feet in the shade and its head in the sun, the common honeysuckle here has reached cultivation nirvana.

Honeyed honeysuckles

Wherever you have hedgerows, walls, and fences, you will find climbing plants: ivies (*Hedera*), clematis, climbing and rambling roses (*Rosa*), and honeysuckles (*Lonicera*). I love them all but the one I would miss most if I were deprived of it would be the honeysuckle. Its perfume is difficult to describe. There is an element of spice – of nutmeg, perhaps, or cloves – and a sweetness that makes you want to bury your nose into its crimson and cream flowers, over and over again. Honeysuckle has fragrance day and night but exudes its scent most powerfully during the evening. Where it is a native plant, it is particularly attractive to indigenous insects.

Most nocturnally scented plants have wonderfully sweet perfume and their long corolla tubes can be pollinated only by something with a long proboscis.

Honeysuckle has no tendrils nor adventitious roots. It relies on twining its stems through the twigs and branches of its host. Jasmine (*Jasminum*) and trachelospermum clamber in the same fashion, and all three create towers of perfume, making them perfect plants for hedgerows, walls, and fences.

Single species or mixed?

Hedges are usually composed of one species of privet (*Ligustrum*) or beech (*Fagus*) or, on numerous occasions, just Leyland cypress (× *Cuprocyparis leylandii*). It is convenient to have a hedge of one type of plant; you can trim it and maintain it more easily than a mixed one. It is assumed that aesthetically it is more pleasing to have just one species, probably because it is taken for granted that a hedge is a backdrop and always thought of as a means of separation or as a foil for other plants.

In contrast, a mixed hedge of indigenous species is a much more desirable alternative and an acknowledgement of how diverse and exciting a hedge can be.

Because most of our indigenous shrubs and trees are deciduous, a native hedge will be a vastly different proposition in spring than in autumn or mid-winter. There will be new shoots on beech with their unfurling, pale green, translucent leaves, frothy blossom from hawthorn (*Crataegus*), and rich red berries and glorious autumn colour from guelder rose (*Viburnum opulus*).

Above – Do these box (Buxus) *bushes with their random yet heavily stylized, cloud-pruned form constitute a hedge? They undulate in an irregular formation through the centre of our "hot" beds, where later they form a background to "hot"-coloured flowers on this side and the other, forming a kind of boundary.*

Opposite above – An existing hedge can be transformed into pure sculpture. Athough still a boundary, it is then much more inviting than a barrier.

Opposite below – My native hedge being newly laid, to waist height. By the following autumn it was taller than me.

162

Ideally, an indigenous hedge should run between gardens, so that both parties can enjoy the benefits. However, even when neighbours are not keen, it is still worth planting one, provided it does not overwhelm the light in their plot. Who knows, when they recognize the benefits, the neighbours may be prepared to tear down the barricades and make use of this wildlife-friendly asset. The more people who join in, the more effective each hedge becomes as wildlife "corridors" are established, along which birds, mammals, and insects can move. Few creatures stay in one place and the longer such corridors become, the more complex are the relationships between wildlife within them.

Diversity is all-important and it is astonishing to realize that within a short run of native hedge there is room for a plethora of indigenous trees. Even the biggest forest trees – oak (*Quercus*) and beech – can be incorporated into a hedge. Oak plays host to an enormous diversity of insects, as well as to the creatures that feed on them. Each element within the hedge will attract creatures specific to its species, and also those with more catholic tastes.

Right – After I have taken a pair of sharp shears to Erigeron karvinskianus *and cut it back really hard – appearing to be brutal at the time – within a few weeks it will be in flower again and will continue to produce a crop of its white and pink daisies right through to the frosts.*

Far right – When we first came to southwest England, I spotted this pretty Erigeron karvinskianus *growing in walls locally. Apparently, when the World Cup was held in Mexico in 1970, this little plant had sown itself all over the stadium, newly built from concrete. It gives you some idea of what a tough character it is and how little it needs in the way of nourishment.*

Opposite – When I built this raised bed, soon after we came to Glebe Cottage, it was as a means to grow some of the plants that would not survive in the heavy clay in other parts of the garden. Over the years, plants have moved in, colonized, and made it their own. Meanwhile, sand lizards often bask on the sun-warmed stones.

Walls as "hedgerows"

A wall can support as much life as a hedge or well-clothed fence. Dry-stone walls offer opportunistic plants footholds to latch on to, cracks and crevices where their roots can delve and explore, be watered and fed by the soil behind the stones, yet with perfect drainage for their rosettes or trailing shoots.

Even walls with mortar, and so no apparent place for flora, can become covered by plants with adventitious roots such as ivy (*Hedera*), which can make a wall its home, growing, flowering, and fruiting, and, incidentally, doing no harm to mortar that is sound.

At the foot of our garden is an old stone wall with lime mortar filling the spaces between the stones. Lichens and mosses cover much of its surface and the little, lime-loving *Asplenium trichomanes* is gradually making its way along the mortar lines.

More than any other factor, it is the aspect of the wall that determines which plants will grow there. Most of the dry-stone walls in the garden here are south-facing. Plants such as *Erigeron karvinskianus*, *Geranium pyrenaicum*, and *Eryngium bourgatii* thrive as soon as they get a foothold. Shadier places are relished by corydalis, ferns, and columbines (*Aquilegia*).

If I had a mind to, our walls could probably offer lewisias a good home. They do not seem to mind what aspect they have, providing they are planted between rocks or the stones of a dry-stone wall.

Opposite – None of our native wild flowers can hold a torch to the foxglove, with its shoulder-high stems (sometimes they are taller than me). Being loaded with belled flowers, all on one side of the stem, they lure in fat bumble bees to transfer their pollen. In one spire the whole life cycle of the flower is apparent, from slender embryonic buds to fattening seed pods.

Below left, centre, and right – It is is incredibly rewarding to sow seed (below left), grow on the plants (below centre), and put them out in the garden when you feel they are large enough to face the big, wide world (below right). Turning the full circle – travelling from seed to plants to seed again – is the essence of gardening – and reminds you of the certitude of nature.

Harbingers of summer

You do not have to stray very far from Glebe Cottage before you come across a foxglove (*Digitalis*). Our hedgerows are punctuated by their tall spires, an annual performance to be enjoyed – exclamation marks in nature's calendar to sign the beginning of summer.

Even earlier, as winter gives way to spring, there is excitement to be had as each woolly rosette advertises a preview of what is to come. Being biennials, they are never in exactly the same spot twice.

Once they have flowered, foxgloves set seed – and lots of it too. A single plant can produce more than a million, possibly two million, seeds, an insurance policy that guarantees the continuous production of plants. Although gardeners should sow foxglove seed that is as fresh as possible (the fresher the seed, the more viable it will be), there is no doubt that in the wild, foxglove seed can remain viable for a long time.

Growing foxgloves yourself is an incredibly rewarding activity. You can save your own seed or buy a packet. Either way there is always more seed than you can use. Although seed can be sown direct, I like to use half-trays of loam-based seed compost, casting the seed very sparsely. Sprinkle a layer of grit over the surface, then water the seed by standing the half-tray in shallow water. Leave outside in a sheltered place, and prick out seedlings when they have their first true leaves.

Eldenhurst, East Sussex
- - - - - - - - - - - - - - - - - -
Helen Yemm's garden at Eldenhurst,
UK, is a miracle. You are lured in through
hedges and fences so thick with climbers
that you forget they are boundaries.
Instead you are distracted, concentrating
on the wealth of beautiful plants, all chosen
with discernment – no room here for the
also-rans. They are put together impeccably.
- -

Case study 8
- - - - - - - - - - - - - -

Hedges to Make Boundaries Disappear

Above – To have a choice of routes in a small garden is unusual, yet as you enter this one, you are presented with options. Should you walk to the right on stones set into grass, alongside a hedge bedecked with exciting climbers, or else go to the left where you can meander through a sea of plants and flowers?

*Opposite – You know you are in for a treat when an entrance, such as the one to the garden at Eldenhurst, is so inviting and alluring. When you step through this gate, under an arch entwined with honeysuckle (*Lonicera*) and Virginia creeper (*Parthenocissus quinquefolia*), you feel that you are entering a very special place. You just have to go in.*

IN SOME WAYS ELDENHURST is an unlikely candidate for a case study in a chapter about hedgerows. There are no hedges in the classical sense of the word, there being no stretches of beech (*Fagus*), privet (*Ligustrum*), or × *Cuprocyparis leylandii*. Yet everywhere at Eldenhurst the use of the vertical is just as pronounced as that of the horizontal. Most gardeners consider the ground and the relationship between plants and that ground, yet the third dimension is of essential importance to the reality they create.

Planting trees and hedges are two ways in which we can introduce vertical spaces, and the latter, as well as fences and walls, can be positioned as boundaries, backdrops, focal points, and "signposts" to describe a route or enclose a space. Thus, even in a small area such as Helen Yemm's garden at Eldenhurst, the use of three dimensions has lent size and volume to the space. It has created mystery – what's behind that fence? – and excitement - what lies around the next corner beyond the fence, the trellis, the structure swathed in climbing plants?

In a small garden it can be difficult to conjure such a sense of excitement, as all too often small areas are predictable. Yet somehow at Eldenhurst, as if by magic, Helen has created a space – indeed, a whole series of spaces – where surprise follows surprise.

169

Helen is a plantswoman through and through. She gardens with verve and originality, backed up with an extensive knowledge of plants and an intuitive understanding of how they work. She knows how to garden and she clearly enjoys it. It is in her blood.

When you walk into any garden, there is always a particular feeling you get from being there. It may change slightly according to the weather (most places seem happier on a sunny day) or the time of year (summer is usually the most ebullient time), but it always exudes its own character, which you can pin down and possibly put into words, as well as its own feeling, which is indescribable but no less real for that. In part, this is down to the place, its geography, its history, and how it was originally conceived. In part, its atmosphere is created by the style of planting, the emphasis that those who have managed the garden have imposed and maybe the contradictions between consecutive garden owners.

In Helen's garden, the overriding feeling is that of joy. She is a practical person, full of sound common sense, but she is also a poet. She loves her plants, adores putting them together, creating ongoing pictures and telling stories with them. It is this rare combination of practical know-how serving a vision for a beautiful garden that gives Helen's garden its ethos.

There are no walls in Helen's garden, apart from those of the house, nor are there "standard" hedges, yet by her use of the vertical, by having plants growing up, lifting our eyes towards the sky, she has designed enclosed places and routes through the garden. The garden is no longer a floor plan but a space we can move through with interest at every level.

The great majority of the plants in Helen's garden are what would be called "cultivated" plants. She chooses the best cultivars, plants that are recognized for their particular qualities; there is nothing run-of-the-mill, yet this is not an exclusive club. If a plant has been identified as being one of the best of its kind, perhaps as having the richest colour among its peers, the longest flowering period, or the ability to stand up for itself without staking, then it deserves a place. There is a lot of snobbery when it comes to selecting plants and too much acknowledgement of the emperor's new clothes – recognizing plants and wanting to include them because they are fashionable and not because they are brilliant. You get the feeling

Opposite – Helen delights in putting plants together and in placing them so that the garden seems bigger than it is. Every opportunity is put to good use to create a garden brimming with energy. You can feel how much these plants love living here, always given the conditions they need and nurtured and cared for at all times.

Below – This delightful rambling rose, Rosa Ferdy, *romping over the greenhouse flowers from early summer to early autumn. The sharp but handsome bracts of Miss Willmott's ghost (*Eryngium giganteum*) has self-seeded through the bed, thereby adding to the richness of the tapestry. Many of the other plants here also have a long season of interest.*

that to qualify for inclusion in Helen's garden you must be special, not necessarily rare but definitely treasured. It is another kind of gardening consciousness that chooses plants just because they are rare. Usually it is the collector ticking plants off the list.

Mixed in among the "cultivated" garden plants in Helen's garden is the kind of melee you would expect to see when out on a country walk, growing at the foot of a hedgerow. In some cases the plants are exactly the same as those you might meet in the countryside: campions (*Silene dioica*), dog daisies (*Leucanthemum vulgare*), and buttercups (*Ranunculus*). Images of some of Helen's little field-edge plantings have been included in the meadow chapter (see pp.248–9), but these plants are not restricted to designated areas; they insinuate themselves into grander schemes within beds and borders.

Although Helen is not a sentimentalist, there is nothing authoritarian about her approach to gardening. Her control is beneficent, even compassionate. She does not seek to control plants.

Above – Every centimetre of space, vertically and horizontally, has been exploited fully at Eldenhurst, yet all the planting is considered. Beds and edges are packed with plants, some of them rare and unusual, others the border stalwarts used by many of us because they are dependable and easy to grow, as well as being beautiful.

Rather, she prefers to let them grow in the way they desire, while she provides the places and the conditions in which they can perform their best. Where it is shady, shade-lovers are planted; in areas of full light, sun-lovers have the limelight.

There is a lovely informality and randomness about the garden born of an understanding of plants and encouraging them to be themselves. Helen has designed so many twists and turns that most areas will experience more than one set of light conditions in a day. Thus hedgerow plants – those tolerant individuals that put up with changing conditions of light and varying amounts of water – cope brilliantly.

The garden at Eldenhurst is designed but never over-designed. At no time do you feel that any part of it is being made to do something it does not want to do. The space itself is a rather odd shape but Helen has made imaginative use of areas rather than seeing them as problems. Meanwhile, the paving is maintained

Above – As you wander along paths, around corners, and past walls, your attention is constantly caught by plants and arrangements, and you momentarily come to a halt, transfixed. Yet, every so often, there is somewhere to stop and sit, as here by the kitchen, with a table and chairs, herbs in a planter, and plants all around.

beautifully, and the lawn and grassy paths are edged crisply, so there are no distractions and nothing to take your attention away from the main focus of the planting.

From every garden I visit, I try to take something "home". Even when the gardens are quite unlike my own, I find that there are still tips that I can adopt, as well as plants that I might be able to experiment with. If your garden has limited space, perhaps with added complications of awkward corners or narrow parts, then Helen's garden can not only help you solve those problems but perhaps persuade you how lucky you are that you are not stuck with a straightforward rectangle. Her wonderful use of space – the way that she deals with hedging and boundaries – is an inspiration.

Whenever possible, be inspired by Helen and the hedgerow to go up in the world and exploit all the space. The third dimension is part and parcel of all our plots and it gives you the chance to grow a host of new and different plants.

Hawthornes
- - - - - - - - - -
There is something wonderfully contrary
about gardening on a perfectly flat,
horizontal site yet concentrating on plants
that explore and exploit vertical space.
At Hawthornes, in Lancashire, UK, the
planting constantly encourages you to look
up and through. It is by no means a large
garden, yet its collection of clematis is truly
encyclopedic and their use is joyful.
- -

Case study 9
- - - - - - - - - - - - - - - - - -

The Ultimate Hedgerow Plant: Clematis

AS YOU APPROACH this garden, and before you push open the gate, clues about the sort of experience you are just about to enjoy announce themselves over the fence and around the gate. This may be a very flat part of Lancashire, UK, but most of this garden is up in the air.

The similarity between their garden and a hedgerow habitat may never have struck Richard or Irene Hodson. They think of their garden as most of us do, as a place to grow the plants they love. They tackle it in terms of creating the best situation to grow their plants and enjoy them.

Richard has the National Collection of *Clematis viticella*, and more than 80 varieties grow here in addition to many other cultivars belonging to different groups – not to mention as many species clematis as Richard can lay his hands on. Species clematis, in particular, but also the vast majority of clematis in general, are hedgerow plants. Wherever they occur, most species clematis are climbers, scramblers, plants that have evolved with trees and shrubs and use them as hosts. To haul themselves up and into the canopy of a tree or to progress along the length of a hedge horizontally, clematis wind their leaf stems around the stems of their hosts. Unlike self-sufficient woody plants, which develop trunks, branches, and twigs

Above – There are no vast architectural structures in the Hawthornes garden but the presence of clematis throughout it, climbing up supports and festooning hedgerows, lends the area a strong vertical accent.

Opposite – Though there are hundreds of wonderful plants throughout Irene and Richard's garden, there is no doubt which species rules the roost. Clematis are Richard's lifelong love.

Above – A purple viticella clematis, C. 'Étoile Violette', easy and trouble-free, meanders through an open trellis framework and provides the background to a different set of plants on each side. Climbing plants that can be viewed from both sides or "in the round" are an enormous asset, especially where space is at a premium.

for support, clematis are dependent on other plants to hold their long stems, which can grow 6m (20ft) or more in one season. They are archetypal hedgerow plants.

Hawthornes is not a huge garden but within it are scores and scores of clematis planted on structures, along walls and fences, in containers, and through trees and shrubs. It is truly clematis wonderland. Too many clematis? Absolutely not. Their forms and colours are so varied, the ways in which they are grown so imaginative, and the manner in which they are combined with a vast array of herbaceous plants (Irene's speciality) and other climbing plants are all so original, so personal, that you could wander around the garden for days without seeing everything.

Richard is no mere collector. He extols the virtues of clematis at every opportunity, not just verbally but practically for all to see. He is constantly inventing new ways in which to show them to best advantage, giving the plants their head and glorying in their outstanding flowers. Thus his National Collection is no museum piece with rigid examples of each sort in regimented rows, ordered,

Above – There are some clematis you just have to allow to grow without restraint, and Clematis fargesii *var.* souleii *is one of them. This Chinese species, which flowers in late summer and into autumn, will twirl its leaf stems around any convenient point, such as the leaves of other plants, wires, or even its own stems. In its turn, it makes a convenient supporting structure for a pretty* C. texensis *with its contrasting, bell-shaped flowers.*

labelled, and standing to attention. Clematis are such anarchists anyway that it would be difficult to imagine anybody stamping their will on them or succeeding in bringing them under control.

Instead, Richard glories in the plants themselves and wants us to do the same. He shares his love for clematis by displaying them in a seemingly endless variety of ways. Most of us grow clematis up walls, providing wires, netting, or trellis for them to wrap their leaves around, extend their stems, and produce their flowers. Yet there are few walls at Hawthornes, apart from those of the bungalow and a shed. Needless to say, all are made use of, but there are also obelisks clothed from head to foot in clematis, as well as free-standing trellis panels, some joined one to another with arches through their centre. Every one of them is clothed in clematis. If there is a tree, it will likely have its own clematis planted a little way out from the trunk, while covering the branches with an extra layer of leaf and flower. Some trees support two clematis, and shrubs, too, are adorned with their luscious flowers in every shade of blue, purple, pink, and crimson, as well as dazzling white.

There are columns and pillars, towers and obelisks, all smothered in varieties of this wonderful plant. Because these free-standing structures are three-dimensional, as you wander around the garden you see them from different perspectives, so the same planting can show another side that is quite different perhaps from the persona it exhibited when first you saw it. Possibly it is one of the deep purple viticellas insinuating itself through a shrub with yellow leaves or flowers, the perfect complement on the other side being the same velvety purple flowers providing the backdrop to sizzling red montbretias (*Crocosmia*), rusty heleniums, and glowing red hot pokers (*Kniphofia*).

You are taken on a trip around the garden, admiring these mouthwatering combinations and not concentrating, as you would in so many gardens, on the beds and borders. Constantly, here, you are looking up and across, as there is height and stature at Hawthornes and all of it in technicolour.

These are all features in the programme but the main event that runs constantly and joins everything else together into one cohesive whole is the perimeter of the garden, where there is more space for some of the most energetic clematis to spread and sprawl. They intermingle with roses (*Rosa*) and shrubs of various persuasions, and gallop upwards and outwards oblivious, of structures en route. The shed is swathed in *Clematis fargesii* var. *soulei*, whose flowers

Above – It is not only shrubs that clematis make use of. This Clematis *'Walenburg' has provided the mouthwatering combination of its delicious, blue-purple flowers intermingled with the yellow blooms of the hymenoxys. Also, its elegant bells contrast attractively with the upturned daisies.*

are dainty and of ivory-white, but whose long stems spread in every direction. This clematis was probably planted way down the hedge but it has no intentions of staying in that place. This is one of the most endearing features about clematis, yet one of its habits that over-tidy gardeners find most difficult to accept.

Some gardeners worry about their clematis. The most vexed question, the one that Richard gets asked time and time again, is: "How do I know how much to prune my clematis?" As far as the numerous cultivars of *Clematis viticella* are concerned, he recommends a very simple solution: the St Valentine's Day Massacre. You may be too busy on that particular date or the weather may be foul, but Richard suggests you go out around that time with your sharpest shears and cut the stems of your viticella clematis, as well as any of the late-flowering species and their cultivars, back to a few buds from ground level. Another pearl of wisdom even easier to follow is: "If it flowers before early summer, do not prune."

Almost every garden needs more height in its planting. We may have hedges, banks, and edges, but growing more clematis up obelisks and arches among herbaceous plants and grasses right in the beds and borders would provide so many more opportunities to emulate what must be one of our richest native habitats: the hedgerow.

Hedgerow plant directory

Digitalis purpurea

Whereas most hedgerow plants are quiet, foxgloves (*Digitalis*) are the exception, with their tall, splendid spires of purple-pink bells. These open in succession, a cunning policy to make sure of pollination. Foxgloves are biennial, so once they have flowered and set seed, they die. Sow seed in the same place two years running for a continuous display.

Symphytum × uplandicum

All comfrey (*Symphytum*) is indispensable for this awkward sort of habitat. It makes long, taproots and brings up minerals, thereby feeding itself and the soil around it. There are many different varieties of comfrey, some with exciting, deep purple flowers, while others are white or pale blue. It is a member of the borage family, so great for bees.

Helleborus foetidus

Stinking hellebore (*Helleborus foetidus*) has leaden, deep green leaves clothing tall stems with heads of pale green, rounded bells, each petal tipped in maroon. As the flowers age, the colour fades and gradually the seed capsules start to turn brown. As they do, each segment of the seedheads splits, revealing black seeds, which are easy to propagate.

Lamium orvala

There is an air of mystery about this handsome dead nettle. Its dark crimson stems are clothed in rich viridian leaves in whorls, which protect hooded flowers of velvet-curtain rose. Every flower boasts its own landing pad for pollinating insects, and a protruding hangar roof, to lure the bee or hoverfly deep inside the cavernous interior.

Ophiopogon planiscapus 'Nigrescens'

This is quite a mouthful of a plant! People often call it black grass for short, although it is actually a member of the lily family. It is often given pride of place in a sunny setting or in containers, but in fact it is a woodlander. Its fine, almost black foliage is wonderful with silver plants, such as a silver lamium.

Melittis melissophyllum

You sometimes find bastard balm (*Melittis melissophyllum*) growing on banks, so it is perfect for a shady corner, or one that has both shade and sunshine. What I love about this superbly long-lived perennial, with its square stems, is that its white flowers, with their pink markings, almost look as though they are sticking their tongues out.

Cardamine pentaphylla

Bittercress (*Cardamine*) are one of my favourite groups of plants. They are relatively seldom used, but I do not know why because they are easy to grow and extremely attractive. They are spring stars, with their digitate leaves and clear mauve flowers borne in bunches. They will grow – indeed, flower prolifically – in really quite dense shade but do not like dry soil.

Actaea simplex (**Atropurpurea Group**) **'Brunette'**

If you are on heavy soil and want something spectacular for autumn in your hedgerow garden, nothing could surpass this actaea. It can reach 2m (6ft) tall. The bead-like buds burst to reveal sweetly perfumed, pure white flowers, and its broad, cut leaves of deepest maroon look dapper from spring right through to autumn.

Lamprocapnos spectabilis

Another plant whose popularity is witnessed by the number of its common names is Dutchman's breeches, lady in the bath, bleeding heart (*Lamprocapnos spectabilis*). This very graceful, elegant plant flowers in spring, becomes dormant by mid-summer, then dies back, but it will return the following year. It can be quite a long-lived perennial.

Rosa canina

Dog rose (*Rosa canina*) clambers into shrubs and trees and uses everything as a host. It opens its beautiful, single flowers during early and mid-summer, typically pale pink, occasionally white, with a great powder puff of anthers in the centre luring insects in, mainly for pollen. Dog rose is a forerunner of many climbing roses.

Aconitum 'Stainless Steel'

The whole aconite family provides welcome colour deep into autumn. Aconites (*Aconitum*) need little light and grow in almost any kind of soil, although being part of the buttercup clan, they do best in strong substantial soils. I love the metallic cast on these rich blue flowers, which goes beautifully well with almost any of the autumn flowerers.

Vinca major

Greater periwinkle (*Vinca major*) is a plant that needs no fuss. It tolerates the most uneven conditions, thriving in the darkest corner or on the sunniest bank. It can cope with soil that is alternately very dry and very wet with amazing resilience. All periwinkles are evergreen and provide solid mats of dark green, slightly glossy leaves, continuously.

Brunnera macrophylla 'Jack Frost'

Big, heart-shaped leaves and sprays of blue flowers make this brunnera a joy in spring. After the flowers have faded, the silver leaves continue to grace the plant into autumn. This is a member of the borage family; it is very tough, very easy to grow, untroubled by pests, and one of the most outstanding plants for a hedgerow or woodland situation.

Anemone × hybrida 'Honorine Jobert'

Along with the berries and changing foliage, autumn brings fresh flowerers to the hedgerows. Chief among them are plants such as Japanese anemones (*Anemone × hybrida*). Tall stems support elegant flowers in pinks and whites. Their roots run just under the surface of the soil, colonizing energetically.

Aquilegia vulgaris

Granny's bonnet (*Aquilegia vulgaris*), from a well-loved genus of plants, is very familiar, due in part to its propensity to set seed, flinging it around and producing lots of new plants. It is very promiscuous too, and you will very often find seedlings that are nothing like the original parents. Most have long spurs and are very graceful, elegant plants.

Convallaria majalis

Lily of the valley (*Convallaria majalis*) has the best spring perfume. Twin leaves of freshest green and stems of creamy white bells opening to pure white make a brilliant combination. This is a native UK plant and it loves to wander around. Like many plants that can become invasive, it is often hard to establish. I could never have too much of it.

Primula vulgaris

In hedgerows, primroses (*Primula vulgaris*) live happily among the leaf litter, moving steadily outwards to take advantage of the humus-rich leaf mould around them. In the confines of gardens, they may need more help. Lift plants as they finish flowering. Tease clumps apart and trim back the roots to 10cm (4in); then plant in compost-enriched soil.

Gillenia trifoliata

A fairy plant, which, like gaura, looks as though a host of butterflies has landed on it. Indian physic (*Gillenia trifoliata*) has branching stems and appears almost like a shrub, although it is herbaceous, dying down each autumn. Before that, it bears splendid autumn foliage in orange, russet, and red. It is almost as attractive then as it is in full flower.

Polygonatum multiflorum

Solomon's seal (*Polygonatum multiflorum*) belongs to the same family as lily of the valley and likes the same kind of conditions. Though there are variegated forms, for me the most elegant and desirable Solomon's seal has simple, plain green leaves. In autumn, it may produce berries of red and black, and foliage in shades of gold and russet.

Clematis vitalba

Clematis has many vernacular names – traveller's joy, old man's beard, virgin's bower – and is found growing in hedgerows and into trees. It loves alkaline soils yet thrives just about anywhere. It has a propensity to smother anything it gets its shoots into – it even strangles trees – hence the "old man" in its common name, which is a reference to the devil.

Euphorbia amygdaloides var. robbiae

Mrs Robb's bonnet (*Euphorbia amygdaloides* var. *robbiae*) is a variant of the species with a very useful habit – it spreads to form dense ground cover. In spring, it is lit by many lime-green bracts and goes on looking good for months. This is a very useful plant for an awkward situation in half-sun and half-shade.

Meconopsis cambrica

I once tried to get rid of Welsh poppy (*Meconopsis cambrica*), thinking there was too much of it, but the following spring I regretted doing so, because this poppy is such a beautiful addition to a hedgerow garden. It has fresh tender foliage and papery flowers, both of which belie its incredible toughness. It is happy in shade or sun or both at different times of day.

Tellima grandiflora

A native of North American woods, fringe cups (*Tellima grandiflora*) is invaluable when it comes to areas of uneven light at the foot of walls or fences. It supplies not only verdant foliage to get the whole spring show on the road, but also bears spires of dainty, palest green, fringed bells – sometimes touched with pink – with a light and haunting fragrance.

wetland

Once upon a time, the British Isles were wetter and there were ditches, lakes and streams, and village ponds. Once agriculture took on its leviathan mantle, they became an inconvenience. Land was drained, ponds were filled in, and the creatures who had evolved with these wetlands went into decline. Yet they are among the most magical – dragonflies and damselflies – and also some of the most fascinating – the amphibians, frogs, toads, and newts.

Transformations to Treasure

WETLANDS SUPPORT some of our most outstanding wild flowers, from the golden globes of kingcups (*Caltha palustris*) to the exotic blooms of water lilies (*Nymphaea*). Without them our natural world is a poorer place. In our gardens, too, water is not just an asset – it also transforms and its effect is magical.

The moment you add the element of water to your garden, its reality changes. It is the extra ingredient that brings enchantment in its wake. It can be tranquil – "as still as a mill pond", reflecting the scene around it and creating a double reality; it can move gently, almost imperceptibly; or it can rage and torrent. Water introduces sound, splashes and bubbles, swishes and gurgles, a new dimension and brings a garden to life. Without its presence our soil would bake and our plants shrivel, but to glorify it for its own sake in the form of a pond, a stream, a sink, a trough, even a bowl, to separate it so we can appreciate it fully, is a hugely rewarding exercise.

The plants that grow in, on, and alongside water are special. They have evolved together with their watery environment so they are perfectly adapted to the special challenges such an environment presents. Most plants forced by flood to face serious inundation for any length of time would simply rot, but our bog-dwellers and paddlers are perfectly at home. It is believed that before the last

Opposite – Our little pond enriches the garden, despite not looking very dramatic. It is from here that most of the frogs and toads that inhabit our garden emanate. On reeds and irises, dragonflies emerge from their nymph stage to assume their adult magnificence. Our pond is a living, breathing hub, full of life and energy. And, as you can see, common duckweed (Lemna minor) also does very well!

Above – Plants such as water lilies are fascinating and initiate so many questions: how do their leaves float on the water surface (see p.211), where do the flowers come from, how far down do their roots go, and how can they distribute seed when they live in water?

Opposite – Water lilies have a compelling attraction at a spiritual level. From Ted Hughes's poem To Paint a Water Lily *to Monet's images at his garden in Giverny, canvas after canvas reveals new aspects to water lilies. Being one of the most ubiquitous of all plants, the water lily is the undisputed ruler of its watery realm, as here on a Scottish loch.*

Ice Age, yellow flag (*Iris pseudacorus*) was a landlubber but, as the glaciers retreated and melted, the water table rose, ground became wetter, and the iris was faced with the sink or swim option. Gradually, yellow flag adapted and so survived. This iris still has a tuberous root but now it is waxy and resilient, and its roots are wiry and can cope with wet conditions. Move it into thin, dry soil and it will wilt. Equally, transfer its relatives that thrive in arid climes to the water's edge and they will sulk and eventually rot and die.

When we bring water into our gardens, there is a whole new vocabulary to learn. The rules for their cultivation and care are slightly different from those for landlubbbers. Plants that live under the water derive their nutrients from that water: for example, pond weed has thin leaf surfaces that can utilize sunlight easily and air-filled cells in their leaves and stems.

The water lily (see p.211) was one of the first flowering plants on the planet. Its evolution and adaptation have been so successful that we are lucky enough to be in a position to offer it and so many other wetland plants a home in our gardens.

Sensory tricks

When very still, water can double our view. Thanks to its power to reflect, it can show us an inverted picture of what we know is real and thereby confuse us by creating a dream-like quality.

Despite gravity, we sometimes wonder what is real, what is not. It is only when a stone is thrown into water and makes a quiet splash and ripple that we recognize for sure which is finite and which reflection – or do we? Two skies, two banks, two Narcissi – surely we can sympathise with the youth who fell in love with his own reflection and, thanks to water, could not distinguish between the real world and a dream.

Though hearing and vision are the senses through which we perceive water, that of touch is involved too. Wet is the opposite of dry, and for the most part our world is a dry one. Trailing your hand in water or paddling your feet in it, especially when the weather is warm and balmy, can be a delicious experience. Even wading around in water when you have got an established pond and jobs to do can be enormous fun.

Above – Water flows evenly over a mini dam, one of a series of steps briefly halting its course. Its passage is more than a trickle, less than a gush, and its accompanying warbling sound can be imagined even when you have never experienced it. Water can make music and play with light in truly magical ways.

*Above – With still water you get double value: two skies for the price of one. A pond's surface partly covered by a sparse forest of water violets (*Hottonia palustris*) is an arresting sight. The slender spires and dainty, white flowers are reflected and the shadow of their underlit stems enriches the bewitching pattern.*

The sound of water is at once soothing and exhilarating, unless it is used for torture. There is a reassurance about the background noise of water as it is the same, day by day – until the flood!

Its force can be unpredictable – and unstoppable. None of the other elements has the power of water. Fire, for example, is ultimately extinguishable. Flood is not, and because all water is connected, it has no bounds. It has no beginning and no end, and because it is continuous, it is an invaluable symbol of the cyclic nature of all we do.

In our gardens, it can provide sounds that underline our experience of being there, noises that we expect to hear. If we want excitement, water can provide it from a fountain or rushing stream. However, most of us need water to engender a sense of tranquillity or serenity or to encourage contemplation. Though we can adjust it, persuade it to run straight down, or place obstacles in its way, it is always the water that is in charge. If we are lucky enough to have it in our gardens, then we must seize the golden opportunity to exploit it and enjoy it; and if not, we can introduce it.

Rills & streams

A ribbon of water running through the garden is always a charming feature. Whether it is a natural watercourse, perhaps a spring-fed stream or a deliberately engineered structure, a rill or narrow canal, it lends the garden a rural character, as well as introducing an element as basic as the soil itself. Water will always babble and gurgle in the background, as though it is holding a conversation with itself.

In nature, rills are narrow channels eroded by water into rock over a long period of time. In gardens, a rill is a construct, often quite shallow and not very wide, that carries water down into a water feature, small pond, or pool, or else the water is pumped back to the top and flows continuously in a circle.

Rills sometimes have formal edges, often of paving stone so that the edging doubles as a path. This has the added advantage that you can hear the water at first hand.

Most rills are clear of plants within the water. The reason plants are usually confined to the banks of rills, rather than used in them, is that they tend to stop the water flowing and clog up the channel. Frequent maintenance would be needed if you were to plant the rill. However, there are exceptions to the no-plant rule, notably the rill that Gertrude Jekyll designed at Hestercombe Court in Somerset, UK, where irises, hostas, and other water-lovers are planted along the bed of the stream.

Right – Here, in the dampest,
shadiest corner of our garden, I am
transplanting a lump of rodgersia into
its new home. Even though it is already
in leaf, it will move successfully. It
is going into a hole that fills up with
water, beside our little stream, so it
will have a constant supply of moisture
although it will never be stagnant.
There is a rich supply of leaf mould too.

*Right – Here, in the dampest,
shadiest corner of our garden, I am
transplanting a lump of rodgersia into
its new home. Even though it is already
in leaf, it will move successfully. It
is going into a hole that fills up with
water, beside our little stream, so it
will have a constant supply of moisture
although it will never be stagnant.
There is a rich supply of leaf mould too.*

*Far right – The handsome foliage of all
rodgersias is particularly striking.*

*Opposite – Each plant in the picture
is in its element. Everything looks
happy and appropriate, and in the
green tapestry that is woven, nobody
is trying to outdo their neighbours. In
the foreground, hostas are in charge,
but despite the fact that their leaf
shapes and scale are similar, there
is enough variety to create a subtly
undulating surface, almost like water.*

Bog-lovers

A boggy area is sometimes easier to achieve than a pond (see p.202).
By excavating an area to 30cm (1ft) or so deep and lining it with
plastic, you can ensure that it will stay damp once the soil is replaced.
The liner can be compost bags slit open and overlaid, or a large piece
of tough plastic with holes punched in it with a garden fork. The idea
is simply to create an area that will not dry out, so the liner does not
have to be waterproof.

Before planting a boggy area, it makes sense to research local
wetland habitats or similar places throughout the world to see what
plants flourish there. Look for bog-lovers to go through the season:
for example, lesser celandines (*Ranunculus ficaria*) – perhaps the
best is *R. f.* 'Brazen Hussy' with its bronze leaves offsetting its golden
flowers. Other members of the buttercup family swiftly follow:
kingcups (*Caltha palustris*) and common European globeflower
(*Trollius europaeus*). The mass of Asiatic primulas that revel in damp
conditions continue the show through spring and into summer with
bog-loving irises, many of them Asiatic too, mixing and mingling.

Foliage is hugely important, and because boggy conditions are
often rich and fertile, this means foliage itself can be huge! Hostas
are a firm favourite, whereas the foliage of rodgersias is lesser
known. They are splendid plants for the bog garden, along with their
close relations, astilbe and filipendula.

Above – *Sometimes having straight edges to your pond can have decided advantages. If the edge of your path is also one side of your pond, you can stand right beside it. If the other edges are obscured by the planting, you become an onlooker gazing into a magical, intimate space. The feeling is enhanced by the planting in the water.*

Opposite above – *A square pond can be used primarily for its geometric shape while still supporting pond life.*

Opposite below – *Iris ensata 'Alba' is one of the most exquisite aquatic irises. Though its elegant flowers last only a few weeks, while they grace the water's edge it is plain to see why they have acquired their vernacular name of butterfly iris.*

Garden ponds

Adding a pond to your garden can change it dramatically. It is a cliché to say that it adds another dimension, yet it does – as well as doing so much more than that.

Deliberately introducing water into your garden is one of the most important gardening decisions you can make. Not only will it extend the vocabulary of plants you can include in your garden story, but it will also enrich the life of your garden in terms of wildlife, attracting a diversity of insects and animals, especially amphibians that you might never otherwise see. Water, especially in the form of a pond, increases the scope of a garden because it is a new element. One of the most satisfying aspects of bringing water into the garden is to enjoy its reflections – you get twice as much for your money and it brings the sky right down to garden level.

To see the sky displayed in the water and watch clouds scudding across its surface is enchanting, while to spot the smooth surface of the water transformed by raindrops, or ripples spread out as a frog decides it is time to explore is very special.

Water is alive and changing constantly. Within a pond the whole year unfurls. As ice melts and frogspawn begins to appear, you know spring is underway. Kingcups (*Caltha palustris*) flower, followed by irises and flowering rush (*Butomus*), and the atmosphere around the pond and the water itself are full of activity. Later, the russet leaves of autumn are reflected in the pond's surface and, eventually, the skeletal branches of mid-winter take over; sometimes the water is blanketed in snow.

Making a pond takes time, effort, and expense, although the biggest outlay is for a good-quality pond liner. To be viable, the pond needs to be a reasonable size, so that a variety of water depths can be included: 1m (3ft) in the middle is desirable, with gently sloping sides and a shelf running around part of the edge on which to grow marginals. There should also be a "beach" – somewhere that birds can come to drink from and where anything that falls into the pond has a chance to climb out.

Although children are intrigued by water, ponds are dangerous places for them when they are young, so fence off the area or cover

Right – Light plays an important role in our gardens, never more so than on plants close to water. Here, the emerging foliage of Rodgersia aesculifolia *is gloriously backlit, so its strong shape is emphasized and the intricate patterns of the underlying structure of ribs and veins are also revealed.*

Opposite – No herbaceous perennials in the whole garden look more glorious than waterside and bog plants. This is especially evident at the height of their summer splendour, when leaves have extended and developed to their peak and flowers are fresh yet lush. The exciting contrasts afforded by different leaf shapes and colours enhance the richness of the pattern and texture.

Below – Here I am planting meadowsweet alongside our little pond, where it will enjoy the damp conditions.

the whole pond with a strong metal grid, or else either wait until they are bigger. A metal grid sounds awful but it can work, and once plants have taken over, much of it is disguised and children can safely enjoy the delights of watching dragonflies emerge and seeing young frogs, newts, and toads moving around the pond margins.

A pond can look odd when positioned in the middle of a manicured lawn, so try to incorporate it in an informal setting, perhaps among wild flowers and grasses or within a cultivated meadow where plants are used naturalistically. Choose an open position, because autumn leaves from overhanging trees can make the water stagnant and change the delicate balance between the water and plants. Also, tree roots can cause havoc with pond liners. The site should be as level as possible – trying to build a simple pond on a slope is a thankless task.

Mark out the area with a hosepipe or length of rope. Remove the top soil layer – if it is turf, stack it back to back in a corner to reuse later. Dig out the pond hole, again keeping the soil – perhaps you can create a raised bed for alpines at the same time. Using a long, rigid plank and a spirit level, keep checking levels as you dig. Remove any stones, line the hole with a layer of sand, at least 5cm (2in) thick, and/or carpet underlay, and lay out your liner, making sure there is at least 30cm (12in) of overhang around all the edges. (It pays to order a bigger liner than you think you will need. Surplus can be used

Above – Plantings that slope down towards the water offer an even greater intensity than those on the flat. Here, the feeling of an amphitheatre is created, and the pond itself is the arena. Tall, fluffy aruncus and stately reeds look on from the banks, while the water reflects the sky, thereby doubling the grandeur.

Opposite – It is the richness of water and wet soil, full of minerals and nutrients, that gives pond and bog plants their energy and their volume. Such plants are never meagre, always generous. Many of their leaves are statuesque – here, those of rhubarb (Rheum) *in the background and darmera at the water's edge are echoed by the water lily* (Nymphaea) *pads.*

to create boggy pockets close by.) The most difficult part of making a pond look natural is disguising the edge of the pond liner. Large, flat stones overhanging by 3–5cm (1–2in) are the best solution. Before filling the pond some people add garden soil or pebbles, so aquatic plants have something to root into.

If you can wait for winter rain to fill the pond or use collected rainwater, this is ideal, as tap water contains chemicals that adversely affect pond life. If you cannot wait, then fill the pond with tap water via a hosepipe and then beg or borrow a bucketful of sludge from a neighbour's successful pond. Ponds should be brimming with life and this murky bucketful should introduce all manner of microlife, as well as eggs and larvae of pond creatures. Just make sure there is no common duckweed (*Lemna minor*) in their pond! Gradually, the water will clear, but you are not after crystal-clear water anyway.

When it comes to planting, you can choose native plants, exotic ornamentals, or a mixture of both. Indigenous plants are the most desirable, as they will support the widest range of native creatures.

Wildlife & water

The flora and fauna of ponds and wetlands are unlike those that frequent other habitats, and their ecosystems are much older – the first life on earth evolved in water. Though each of our gardens can make only a small contribution to wetland habitats, taken together they constitute a vitally important resource for endangered wildlife. How privileged we are not only to be able to take steps to redress any imbalance, even though each step is ever so tiny, but also to enjoy the special creatures that depend on water for their very existence, by ensuring we provide the appropriate plants and other conditions right here in our own gardens.

The life cycle of most pond creatures is intimately tied to the water itself, yet many of them spend only part of their lives in it. Dragonflies that emerged on the rushes and reeds beside the water's edge will spend hours hunting around our borders, and those same borders provide dense cover for the frogs, toads, and newts that were this season's tadpoles. Thus pond life is very esoteric and endlessly fascinating.

*Above – This striking picture with its horizontal emphasis comprises strata of plants, as well as the water itself, creating layer upon layer of textural interest. A dense green background is the foil for a regiment of yellow flags (*Iris pseudacorus*). Rushes line the edge of the pond, and the water itself is embossed with water lilies (*Nymphaea*) *and a host of water violets (*Hottonia palustris*).*

*Opposite – As far as wildlife is concerned, nothing beats a native plant in its element. Here, the tall, vertical spikes of purple loosestrife (*Lythrum salicifolium*) *continue the season for foraging insects.*

208

The importance of floating leaves

In any pond, if life below water is to succeed, there need to be plants with floating leaves, to create places for creatures to hide and to offer shade. Water lilies (*Nymphaea*) are the most obvious choice. If you have a really big pond, white water lily (*N. alba*) is ideal but it can spread hugely, so beware. Another possibility – yellow pond lily (*Nuphar lutea*) – is on a much smaller scale and bears glorious, golden, cup-shaped flowers, but it, too, can eventually become a thug.

The ways in which the water lily has evolved are fascinating. Its roots gather nutrients from the soupy sludge at the bottom of the pond, thereby sustaining the plant. Simultaneously, the stems that support the giant floating leaves have a series of hollow tubes within them that carry oxygen to the roots. Though the gigantic leaves look quite smooth on their upper surfaces, when you turn them over, you see a complex web of radiating ribs with interconnecting side ribs. This network supports the leaf, making it incredibly strong and enabling it to support itself on the surface of the water, despite its great size. It was this structure that inspired Joseph Paxton's 1851 designs for Crystal Palace, in London.

Water lilies inhabit every continent apart from Antartica, and many are from tropical climes. There are scores of ornamental water lilies from which to choose. Some will grace a small or large pond or even a water garden in a trough – just make sure of their hardiness and their eventual extent before you bring them home.

Opposite – Water lilies are surely one of the most iconic flowers in the world. Even those who have never come across a water lily face to face can picture it in their mind's eye: the large, round leaves extending over the water's surface, a foil for the pristine, many-petalled flowers. Reflection means the effect is always doubled.

Below left – Lily pads are an astounding feat of evolutionary engineering. For much of the time they float contentedly on the water's surface but when overcrowded can lift themselves out of the water as they jostle for space.

Below right – All water lilies grow rapidly. Though they create an impression of calm and peace, they are far from being static plants. Like their watery surroundings, they are constantly on the move.

Wind in the Willows

In the heart of Buckinghamshire, UK, is an idyllic, 1.2-ha (3-acre) garden, verdant and peaceful, where water holds sway. The plantings are rich and generous and the garden exudes tranquillity. It is difficult to believe that the busiest motorway in the country is just a few kilometres away.

Case study 10

Exploiting Water's Wonderful Wanderings

Above – Red-lacquered Japanese bridges are meant to stand out. They are striking in their own right and also in tune with their watery surroundings, affording views up and down the stream.

Opposite – The garden is rich in views and vistas, but visitors are not just onlookers. They are drawn in, as participants. Here, at the confluence of two streams, whether they are going towards the house or coming from it to explore the garden, visitors are invited to cross the stream.

WIND IN THE WILLOWS is one of the most tranquil gardens you could visit. It is bounded by a river and a mill stream, so the garden owes its character predominantly to water, even though there are areas of woodland and traditional plantings of shrubs, trees, and perennials.

Few of us have the asset of running water in our gardens. We may be able to dig ponds, perhaps even a short rill, but to have water "in transit" – actually passing through our land with all its bustling and babbling, or sometimes with quiet, more tranquil sections – is rare indeed. That Ron James appreciates what he possesses (this is, after all, the reason why he chose the property) is evident because he has done everything to work with the water, to respect it, enhance it, and make use of it. His labours have resulted in an outstanding garden.

Introducing water into your garden is a straightforward – be it sometimes arduous – process: a pond can be dug and water features created. Though very few of us will ever be able to re-create the scenario that Wind in the Willows enjoys, there are many aspects of this garden that we can emulate, even when the water in it is still.

Plants are of primary importance here. Nonetheless, there is the feeling that everything serves the whole, making a cohesive garden with a strong identity.

*Above left, centre, and right –
The importance of light and the extra
dimension that water can add are
exemplified in these three beautiful
images of Jonathan's. The white edge
of the variegated hostas (above left)
is emphasized as light hits their flat
surfaces, contrasting with the linear
pattern of the iris leaves. Backlit irises
appear dark against the brilliance of
the water (above centre), while the
emerging foliage of* Darmera peltata
*creates a striking pattern among
irises (above right).*

*Opposite – At the water's edge,
a fine stand of* Iris pseudacorus
*'Variegata' overlooks the stream. The
impact of its elegant, sword-shaped
leaves is doubled, being mirrored
in the gently flowing water, whose
soft movement blurs the edges of the
foliage's reflection.*

*Overleaf – Every element in this scene
contributes to a feeling of tranquillity,
from the arrogant verticals of primulas
and irises to the horizontal water with
its muted reflections.*

Predominantly the garden is green, and it is this overwhelming verdancy that sets the tone and forms the background for the real focus of the garden, its *raison d'être*: water. Bounded on one side by a mill stream (part of the land was originally watercress beds) and on the other by the River Misbourne, the garden is prescribed by the water and you are never far from it. Along the edges of both watercourses, plantations of Asiatic candelabra primulas and irises line the banks, self-seeding and colonizing so that all formality is lost. In other areas, the grass comes right down to the water's edge, enabling visitors to enjoy the vista of the water gently rippling by. Overhead, breezes whisper through the trees, the movement of their leaves creating areas of dappled light, constantly changing and enhanced by the water.

For me, the essence of any garden is the fit between the place and its plants. Though I can appreciate formality, I love gardens that reach a "state of grace", where nothing jars or clashes and everything looks as though it were meant to be a natural scene.

Only part of the Wind in the Willows garden is designated as "wild", yet nothing about it seems formalized or contrived. It creates the impression of a natural planting, somewhere that just grew like that. Plants may self-seed, clumps of iris and hosta may spread and colonize, but a picture like this does not make itself. It takes a great deal of careful thought and planning and an intimate knowledge of plants.

*Right – Asiatic primulas in a moisture-loving melee with shuttlecock fern (*Matteuccia struthiopteris*) relish this damp site and will pop up here and there of their own volition. Sedge (*Carex*) provides a backdrop as do the lemon globes of common European globeflower (*Trollius europaeus*), making another winning combination. All will increase well and are easy to maintain.*

Opposite – This streamside and soggy bank are home from home for candelabra primulas. These glorious plants will self-seed profusely when they are happy, and they make loads of seed. As each carousel of flowers starts to develop seed, the stem lengthens, producing another ring of flowers and so on and so on. Eventually, there may be as many as eight or nine rings of flowers on one stem.

Whether it is at the edge of a watercourse or around a pond in a suburban back garden, the plants that are going to thrive are the same. They have all evolved to deal with water at their roots, sometimes permanently, in other cases seasonally. They have devised different strategies to cope and make the most of their watery environment. Asiatic primulas, for example, have a network of fine feeding roots that take in nutrients and pass them on to leaves, stems, and flowers. Their leaves are large and need masses of water to expand; their growth, as with so many moisture-lovers, is rapid. The roots of yellow flag (*Iris pseudacorus*) have also adapted to water, evolving from being a land-dweller to becoming a plant that can survive not only damp soil but also total immersion. In the shallow margins, but still with roots below water level, a multitude of plants will grow: for example, kingcup (*Caltha palustris*), with its glorious golden chalices, and handsome bog bean (*Menyanthes trifoliata*), with its oval leaves and pretty, starry flowers.

In any watery environment, be it pond or streamside, one of the most essential elements is plants with vertical leaves – rushes,

Opposite and below – Among water's most important gifts to our gardens is its ability to reflect, to create another world, an upside-down, mirror image of the plants within it and at its edge. As well as reflecting plants, water reminds us of the weather, the time of day, the season, and brings the sky right into the heart of our gardens.

sedges, and irises – which provide a ladder for aquatic larvae to climb when they are ready to transform into their airborne incarnation. Japanese rush (*Acorus gramineus*) and its variegated version are ideal here, while flowering rush (*Butomis*) – not a rush at all but a member of the family – has straight stems and heads of delightful, starry flowers. Wind in the Willows is rich in such plants with vertical foliage. If there are no rushes, you will not be able to enjoy dragonflies or damselflies, watching transfixed as they perform their glorious aerobatic displays – surely reason enough to introduce water into your own garden.

If you want a garden full of frogs and toads, where dragonflies zoom over the flowerbeds, there is no time like the present to start making changes to your own garden. These alterations need not be huge or expensive. The more varied the conditions in and around the water that you introduce, the greater the range of wildlife you will attract. The most wildlife-friendly ponds, streams, and bog gardens are composed of native plants. You may decide to concentrate on them, or mix them with exotics, as Ron James has done here, or else, to try to achieve maximum colour and effect, using just exotics.

If possible, there should be oxygenators, such as *Ceratophyllum demersum*, to keep the water clean and prevent it from becoming stagnant. In moving water this is never a problem. One of the most unsightly problems in a pond is the production of algae and blanket weed during the summer months. Oxygenators help, but if life below water is to succeed, there need to be plants with floating leaves, too, to create places for creatures to hide and to shade areas of the water. Water lilies (*Nymphaea*) are the most obvious choice, while pickerel weed (*Pontederia*) is an extremely attractive plant whose long leaves – like rectangles with their corners trimmed – float on the surface of the pond, interrupted here and there by spikes of bright blue flowers. Water hawthorn (*Aponogeton distachyos*) has delicate spikes of dainty, white blossom and spreading leaves.

Around the edges of the pond, shallow shelves or ledges diversify the planting opportunities, and by using butyl under the level of the surrounding garden, you can create a bog garden too (see p.201). Using humus-rich soil over the butyl means you can grow a huge range of Asiatic candelabra primulas. All are totally hardy and look spectacular in large drifts in a kaleidoscope of colour, ranging from magenta, red, orange, and yellow through to coral, pale pink, and lilac. If you want to see them in all their glory, there is nowhere better than along the edges of the streams at Wind in the Willows.

221

Marwood Hill occupies a unique and highly desirable situation in a steep valley close to Barnstaple, North Devon, UK. To the west is the Taw estuary; the sea and Ilfracombe lie just a few kilometres due north. The valley in which Marwood Hill Garden is sited is deep and provides shelter. As the garden has matured, it feels more and more a part of the landscape.

Case study 11

Lakes, Streams, & Boggy Places

Above – Around the lakes there are plenty of places to enjoy the wide vistas of the hillsides sloping down towards the water and lending a panoramic background to Marwood Hill.

Opposite – These stretches of grass alternate with densely planted areas rich in visual interest, and they are ideal not just to engage the horticultural spirit but also to provide a brilliant habitat for wildlife.

MARWOOD HILL is a big garden, 8ha (20 acres) and still expanding, yet it has considerable relevance to the home gardener in its plantings, design, and, especially, its use of water.

I have to confess – this is more of a proclamation than a confession – that Marwood Hill is one of my favourite gardens and, though I do not profess to know it intimately, I have been lucky enough to see it develop over the past 35 years. It is only half an hour's drive from Glebe Cottage, but my visits have been too few and too far between. Of course, Marwood Hill was in existence long before we moved here. The garden was started in the 1950s by a local doctor, Jimmy Smart, and from a relatively modest start he continued to enlarge it both geographically and horticulturally.

People who knew Dr Smart and his pioneering ways sometimes joked that he would press on up the valley, colonizing more and more ground until he got to the sea. But he needed more ground to house his ever-increasing collection of plants gathered from friends and fellow gardeners, not only in the UK but also from all over the world – he was constantly travelling and collecting. Malcolm Pharaoh was his head gardener from the 1970s and, since Dr Smart's death, has continued to run the place with the same ethos – plants have always been the priority.

Above – Alongside the stream, areas of the bog garden broaden out into jungle-like spaces, where huge clumps of perennials vie with each other for moisture and space. It is a happy competition, though, with no losers.

Opposite – You may never have appreciated astilbes until you have seen them at Marwood Hill. Malcolm has travelled vast distances to locate as many varieties, cultivars, and selections as he can to swell the ranks of Marwood's National Collection of astilbes. Almost exclusively from east Asia, astilbes occur in bogs and beside water, making them ideal for water gardens.

Overleaf – In this secluded corner, plants are allowed to be themselves and mingle happily at the water's edge.

A natural stream that ran through the valley was harnessed by Dr Smart to create three lakes. In between the lakes, the stream runs its natural course and either side of it are inspiring plantings full of hostas, irises, primulas, and ferns. There are ligularias and aruncus, and throughout these boggy areas astilbes lift the plantings with their light, fluffy tone. Alongside the biggest lake, the National Collection of astilbes is magnificently displayed, each variety cheek by jowl with the next, yet all making a cohesive statement.

Because in some places the sides of the streams are quite steep, any view of the plantings is foreshortened, so it seems even deeper and richer. This is an idea that could be copied on a domestic scale. Even if the site is fairly flat, there is no reason why the sides of a pond could not slope gradually down to the water level. In areas of high rainfall or where flooding is a problem, there needs to be an overflow at the level of the water, but it would be worth this trouble to be able to pack in the plants and create the same lush effect.

At Marwood Hill, great thought is given not just to the varieties included but also to scale. Many bog plants have big leaves and

Opposite – To create such a naturalistic scene involves hard work. Huge clumps of astilboides and rodgersia, irises and ferns, mingling with the soft inflorescences of lady's mantle (Alchemilla), seem always to have been growing here. They are happy. The stream meanders through, gently flowing this way and that, and leads us into a magical landscape.

Below – At one point the stream veers around a bend encompassing a fairytale space, where an expanse of vegetation, long grass, and primulas creates an enchanting interlude, while glimpses of the landscape beyond beckon you onwards.

luscious growth. In a large garden such as this, broad brush strokes can be used. A limited space is more challenging, as the plants will grow in the same way and to the same dimensions. One solution might be to include everything but simply reduce the numbers used of each variety. A better way would be to cut down the number of different varieties but still make a bold statement. Water gardens should be nothing if not generous, and it is counterproductive to miniaturize everything.

There is plenty of undulation in the plantings at Marwood Hill, and these are not just at their edges as they follow the course of the stream or the contours of a lake's edge. Malcolm Pharoah has adopted the excellent device of creating surprise and holding interest by introducing waves of taller plants or clumpier plants or spikes from front to back of the planting – in other words, from the water's edge through to the outside edge, where the planting meets lawn or path. Where plants are used to create recesses through taller

Above left – Each different view at Marwood Hill presents its own cameo, encouraging us to study and admire the planting or perhaps concentrate on a particular subject. Here, green predominates – the deep glowing green that only water brings. A ligularia with broad, glossy leaves contrasts with the much-divided fronds of its neighbour – a bonny clump of shuttlecock fern (Matteuccia struthiopteris).

Above right – It is usually the foliage of rodgersia that is celebrated but here the full flowers show its pretty side.

planting, exciting glimpses are offered into the pond or water's edge from the other side, through to the view beyond. Another advantage of this sort of "wave planting" is that when something is not in flower – whether it has finished or not yet started – your eye is always led on to the next excitement in the planting.

Throughout these boggy areas, water is glimpsed as it gurgles along the bed of the stream, over shale, around stones, dropping gradually until it meets another lake or broadens out around a glade of dawn redwood (*Metasequoia*). Eventually it ambles on into the countryside beyond. It would be difficult to emulate this scenario in a domestic garden, but the idea of having a wide, boggy area where moisture-loving plants could seed and spread is an attractive one. You could create a broad boggy area anywhere that has fairly level ground (see p.201). Instead of a stream running through it, simple paths could be made with stepping stones, so you could walk through your plantation of primulas or fritillaries (*Fritillaria*).

Above left – Differences in scale always add contrast to any garden picture.

Above right – The fluffy heads of the astilbe emphasize the straight, sword-like foliage of the irises.

You might wonder at first what relevance such an extensive garden might have to your own, but everywhere you look at Marwood Hill there are ideas that can be carried home – ways of using and combining plants that might be adopted in your garden. Here, you are constantly reminded of the unique qualities that water can bring to a garden, whether it be in ponds, alongside streams, or in boggy places, and of the wealth of plants that enjoy paddling, floating, or just living in moist soil.

You are conscious of the special nature of the plants themselves. Yet, simultaneously, Marwood Hill encourages you to think about settings, creating pictures, and the importance of immersing yourself, figuratively though not literally, in the world of water. In this garden, your interest is constantly moving between the bigger picture and the detail, from the views to the plants. It can be enjoyed on so many different levels, offering ideas and inspiration about using watery environments to seasoned and novice gardeners alike.

Wetland plant directory

Lysichiton americanus

It is the combination of the glorious, big, golden spathe and the central spadix that makes yellow skunk cabbage (*Lysichiton americanus*) both handsome and amusing, especially when the spathe has faded away. The spadix actually contains the tiny flowers, but the spathe attracts the insects to pollinate it, which it does through means of smell.

Caltha palustris

The great golden chalices first thing in spring are a joyous sight. You know the winter has passed. Kingcup or marsh marigold (*Caltha palustris*) grows right in the water, submerged, and, with its glossy, kidney-shaped leaves and shiny, buttercup flowers, it makes a real splash of bright yellow in the countryside or garden.

Carex elata 'Aurea'

I would not be without Bowles' golden sedge (*Carex elata* 'Aurea') in any location where the soil is damp all day. It is perfect as a marginal, or in a bog garden. Like all sedges, the male flowers are at the tip of the stems and the female ones are halfway down – a cunning device to ensure pollination. It will seed itself around and the seedlings come true.

Ligularia

Almost all of these striking plants come from Asia, with the exception of a few Europeans. They have various shapes and sizes, mainly yellow or orange flowers, and many produce handsome foliage, which sadly slugs love. They belong to the daisy family, Asteraceae, as can be seen by close inspection of their flower spikes, and are invaluable for wet or damp places.

Primula florindae

This distinctive plant is from Tibet and is one of my favourite primulas. There are red, orange, even russet-brown forms of giant cowslip (*Primula florindae*), but I think this clear pale yellow is the most effective in a garden setting. The buds are covered in farina (white flour), and the flowers open in succession. It is an easy plant to grow from seed.

Trollius

Globeflowers (*Trollius*) adore wet soil and heavy clay. Common European globeflower (*T. europaeus*), with its pale lemon globes, is probably my favourite. There are others with bigger flowers, some New Zealand globeflowers, which open wide showing their stamens, but to me one of the plant's charms is that those petals are never parted.

Mimulus guttatus

Monkey musk (*Mimulus guttatus*) used to be a very familiar flower, and was imported from the US at an early date. At certain times during its cultivation it seems almost to have disappeared, yet will come back with a vengeance. Its cheeky, bright yellow flowers look almost too big for the dainty growth but it is a robust plant, which just gets on with growing.

Rheum palmatum

Chinese rhubarb (*Rheum palmatum*) is a very handsome rhubarb from quite a big family of plants. It grows as high as 1.8–2.1m (6–7ft) to the top of its flower spikes and its leaves are immense. In the best form, they are rubescent, stained with red and crimson around the edges, but the buds in spring are almost rude as they come through the ground.

Rodgersia aesculifolia

If you want big, handsome foliage, nothing could be better than this. The leaves have a tough, leathery, almost polished texture, and are red when they emerge, become green in summer, and then colour up again later. It has big spikes of astilbe-like flowers, deep crimson-red in some forms. Unlike some big-leaved plants, slugs seem to leave it alone.

Iris pseudacorus

Yellow flag (*Iris pseudacorus*) is a familiar plant all over the northern hemisphere. It has straight stems, slender, sword-like leaves, and characteristic, bright yellow flowers. Apparently, it adapted to living in or under water when the glaciers melted after the Ice Age. It is an important plant for insects and for emerging dragonflies and caddisflies.

Gunnera manicata

Not a plant for the faint-hearted, nor for those with small gardens, but if you have the space, what could be more striking than one plant of this beautiful gunnera? It has enormous leaves, so big you could stand underneath them when it is fully grown, and these strange flowers, whorl after whorl, up stout stems. It will grow in the water or beside it.

Aruncus dioicus

Goatsbeard (*Aruncus dioicus*) can be a pretty architectural plant when it gets going, but only when it is grown in damp conditions. It has huge, lax plumes of creamy white flowers. Its foliage in autumn colours up brilliantly well too – an added advantage.

Primula sieboldii cultivar

This exquisite Japanese primula spends three-quarters of the year underground preparing for its wonderful vernal show. When it does burst through the ground, there is nothing like it. Fresh, delicate, green leaves form the base of the plant and from them rise short stems with almost fairy-like, primula flowers above them. It loves a moist place.

Filipendula ulmaria

Meadowsweet (*Filipendula ulmaria*) flourishes in damp ditches from where its lovely froth of pretty, white flowers reaches into hedgerows. Its soft scent is glorious, reminiscent of a mid-summer evening's stroll. The eye-catching, strong dark green leaves change to shades of red, orange, and russet in autumn.

Osmunda regalis

This has a truly regal bearing, growing to 1m (3ft) plus and several metres wide. Royal fern (*Osmunda regalis*) is unlike most ferns in that it bears its spores on separate fronds. These are instantly recognizable, and every plant contains both fertile and sterile fronds. If you have the room, it is well worth putting in one big feature plant of royal fern.

Menyanthes trifoliata

Being the only one in its genus, bogbean (*Menyanthese trifoliata*) is rather a special plant. It develops great thick, spreading roots – rhizomes really – which form mats under the water. Then it puts up shoots, with big, solid leaves divided into three parts, hence *trifoliata*. The leaves make a wonderful contrast to the delicacy of the feathery flowers.

Geum rivale

Water avens (*Geum rivale*) has delightful, nodding heads of coral-coloured, almost apricot flowers with a decided brown calyx. There are different sorts of geums but any with *rivale* in their name are suitable for growing in a bog, beside a pond, or in any damp area, even with heavy soil. In such places, the plant will thrive and go on year after year.

Nymphaea

Water lilies (*Nymphaea*) are perfectly in tune with their habitat and have an incredibly clever way of achieving pollination. Insects are lured into the centre of the flower, which closes and pulls them under the water. Unable to escape, they pollinate the flowers. In the morning, the flower rises out of the water, opens up, and the insects escape.

Persicaria bistorta

There is a certain elegance to this workaday plant from Europe and northern Asia, with its dense spikes of small, pale pink flowers and its copious leaves. It is very tolerant, but if it were able to choose its position, it would invariably be in a damp place. It is lovely in a bog garden and makes beautiful, big clumps beside a pond.

Astilbes

Easy-to-grow astilbes flourish in damp, boggy conditions and build up into stupendous clumps. They come in a great variety of flower forms and colours – everything from white to deep purple and shades of pink and lilac in between. They have become one of the most popular of garden plants. The foliage is handsome too, very shiny and much divided.

Iris ensata 'Rose Queen'

Japanese butterfly iris (*Iris ensata*) is so-called because of the delicacy and lightness – the floatiness – of the falls of its lower petals. In recent years, there have been many attempts to create new cultivars, some of which are big and gaudy and so lose the point of the plant, which is its grace and elegance. It is perfect as a marginal, and you can grow it in water.

Lysimachia salicaria

Purple loosestrife (*Lysimachia salicaria*) has narrow leaves and tall spikes of purple flowers. There are many garden hybrids now, some of them with pink and white flowers, and various shades of lavender, but it is the purple one that makes the most impact. It will grow in or near the water and will seed around all over the garden.

Primula japonica

The Japanese candelabra primulas include many different species but all have the same habit. The one in the photograph is a particular favourite of mine, a pale pink seedling from an original white form called *Primula japonica* 'Postford White'. It loves any damp place and is easy to propagate. Collect seeds from the first whorls of flowers and sow immediately.

meadow

Most meadows exist in our imaginations, a composite image/idyll composed of a Laurie Lee poem or, more prosaically, of a shampoo advertisement. Very few of us have been lucky enough to wander around in a real meadow. Yet meadows are so much a part of our history and culture that we imagine we must know how that feels. We yearn to walk in one, to sit among the wild flowers, buttercups (Ranunculus)*, and dog daisies* (Leucanthemum vulgare)*, poppies* (Papaver)*, and cornflowers* (Centaurea cyanus).

Re-creating the Myth

Opposite – I relish collecting the dead flowers from daylilies (Hemerocallis) *in the brick garden at Glebe Cottage. The simple beauty of the pale fresh flowers of* H. lilioasphodelus *on an early summer morning, its gentle perfume filling the air, creates moments of unalloyed joy, and the flowers' very ephemerality makes the encounter even more precious.*

MEADOWS WERE TRADITIONALLY grazed by cattle then cut for hay, which was turned in the summer sun, a fragrant mix of sweet vernal grasses and wild flowers and herbs, and then stored for winter feed. It must have been nearly as good as the real thing, the fresh grass, chewed and chomped, a reprise of summer in the middle of cold, short days.

No one is suggesting that we all convert our gardens to hay meadows or cornfields, but both these locations have a great deal in common with some of the scenarios we create in our gardens. They are relevant, worthy of contemplation and close study.

Meadows are essentially open, usually in full light. They contain a community of like-minded plants – classically, grasses and perennial herbaceous plants – that mingle and mix in an easy relationship. Originally, in conjunction with the animals themselves, meadows would have been managed by the farmers who owned the land. Hay meadows were permanent; they were not ploughed and reseeded every few years. They were composed of plants that were made to live together and needed no artificial fertilizers, no chemicals.

Our garden equivalent of the meadow is a bed or border packed with herbaceous perennials, growing cheek by jowl with

239

Above – In our "hot" borders Papaver *'Beauty of Livermere' or, as we must now call it so unromantically,* P. Goliath Group *'Beauty of Livermere', turns up the heat at the start of the season.*

*Opposite – Corn poppy (*Papaver rhoeas*) is seldom seen nowadays thanks to zealous use of agricultural weedkillers, but when its vibrant red flowers thrust themselves forward at the site of some new road excavation, it is a delight for everyone.*

grasses. The major difference is that our borders, to a greater or lesser extent, are planned rather than dictated by an agricultural requirement (necessity), and our management of them is much more elaborate. We replant, divide, add bulbs, sprinkle seed. We collect seed too and cut back plants. We want a garden that gives pleasure from first thing in spring, on through summer, and into autumn and, if possible, into winter too.

The plants we use exude a sense of the meadow. In many cases, they or their close relatives come from meadows and prairies in temperate regions all over the northern hemisphere. We have the privilege of putting them together, trying to think of how plants will develop and how that can be exploited and thereby create our own pictures – or films – for our plantings will change constantly with the light, the season, and the weather.

There are as many different kinds of meadow as there are gardens, and if we acknowledge the lessons these beautiful places have to teach us when choosing and combining our plants, we can indeed create magical places of our own. Are not we lucky?

Right and far right – In the Glebe Cottage brick garden, so-called because the paths are made from bricks, the area is separated into a series of small beds (right). When viewed as a whole, they are fairly homogenous and one of the plants that lends continuity is a bulb – quamash (Camassia quamash) (far right).

Perennial meadows

The archetypal meadow is an amalgam of perennial flowers and grasses. Its composition varies according to its soil and situation and, to an extent, its geography. The same should be true for our "meadow" plantings. Meadows and prairies are necessarily made up of wild flowers and grasses, not only indigenous but also often local.

There may be no wild flowers in our garden meadows but it is the spirit of the meadow we are are trying to capture. In fact, following rules and dictums is against the essence of meadow planting. Our plants are selected because they are as close to the traditional species as possible – this means they are likely to be robust and healthy and so need less mollycoddling. Though there will be times when we intervene, it should be a question of adjustment and fine-tuning.

There are as many kinds of meadow planting as there are gardeners practising it. Thank goodness we are all different. A few guidelines, however, stop the whole process becoming too anarchic. Tough, reliable perennial plants, real stalwarts, must form the basis of all our plantings, but what we choose and how we put them together are what makes our meadow plantings our own. What may work perfectly in one year may fail in another, but along the way there are unexpected surprises, unimagined effects, and accidental loveliness that make the whole thing worthwhile and add a new dimension to our gardening efforts.

Opposite – There are no worries about lack of unity in this meadow. Although it is managed, and therefore not strictly wild, nonetheless everything here is perfectly at home; it belongs. Its constituents are in balance, yet it does not create a feeling of torpor – quite the opposite. It has an energy and dynamism few garden schemes could equal.

Opposite – Deliberate "backbone" planting and the acknowledgement and acceptance of how plants self-seed give this scheme a perfectly naturalistic air. Gardening is not nature, but if our choice of plants and the way we put them together are guided by what we see in wild places, then our plots should have an uncontrived and happy feel.

*Below – Dog daisy (*Leucanthemum vulgare*) for some is a ubiquitous wild flower that immediately bestows on a planting a feeling of simplicity and naturalness. Though it is a perennial, it will seed itself around, and its population map (profile) constantly changes. This mobility and unpredictability are welcome characteristics in meadow planting.*

Nurturing the feeling

Must a planting be composed of wild flowers or at least contain a percentage of them to qualify as a meadow? The simple answer is that it does not matter. How it feels and the atmosphere it creates establish its credentials.

There may not be a single wild flower present yet a meadow feel has nonetheless been established. Most successful schemes rely on plants that are so close to their natural roots that they combine happily together and are totally *comme il faut* alongside native plants. The latter do not have to arrive by chance – though often it is these opportunistic adventurers that are the real catalysts in a successful scheme.

Wild flowers are very often straightforward to propagate and can often be sown *in situ*. All meadow plantings can look contrived initially, but despite the fact that plants are earthbound, they do move, and as plants begin to wander and self-seed, more naturalistic results establish themselves.

Transformation into a meadow area

When we were forced to close our nursery a few years ago, almost a hundred railway sleepers were rescued from the site and used to make a series of raised beds towards the foot of the garden, just before you get to the gypsy caravan. They are about 1.2m (4ft) wide and have level paths around them. Though they are separate beds, when it came to planting them, we wanted to design a scheme that would meld, so that during the growing season you could look down on them or up into them and feel that this was a unity, a whole. That reality was created in part by using the same plants in each of the beds – all were and still are herbaceous perennials – and each bed is underplanted with spring bulbs: *Galanthus* 'S. Arnott', *Iris* 'Katharine Hodgkin', and a dainty, white *Narcissus* 'Petrel'.

We succeeded in our idea that it should have a naturalistic, meadow feel. From spring until deep into autumn, the overall impression is that of a meadow. By late spring, the edges of the beds are obliterated, and when you walk between them, you are in the midst of a meadow – not as an onlooker but as a participant.

Few people would find themselves with a similar scenario and I hope for their back's sake they will not have to lug around quantities of sleepers, yet making a meadow planting in a raised bed, whatever its size, is entirely possible in any setting rural or urban. Lack of space or having no soil need not mean you must forego your meadow. We used compost imported from our old nursery beds.

Above left, centre, and right – Digitalis purpurea *'Sutton's Apricot' (above left) seeds itself among* Astrantia *'Roma' (above centre). Later, there are* dierama *(above right) and grasses.*

Opposite – *Here are our raised meadow beds in early summer. There is a seat along one of the paths, so you can sit in the midst of flowers. The colour scheme is predominantly pinks and whites, with splashes of crimson.*

Mini meadows

Some of you must have had the same thing happen in your plots as frequently happens in mine. Plants will put themselves together, seeding into the gravel or at the edge of beds where feet seldom tread and creating miniature gardens without any input from me. Most years there is one such "happening" on the track between the sunny and shady sides of my garden, where meadow cranesbill (*Geranium pratense*) with flowers of softest blue intermingles with self-seeded bronze fennel (*Foeniculum*), both rising up from a mat of *Geranium × oxonianum* and lady's mantle (*Alchemilla mollis*). Every year, it is different; there are new players in the entertainment, but always the stage sets are better than anything I could create.

There has to be management of such schemes, though, especially if you are short of space, but they require adjustments with a light touch. First consideration is having the right plants to create meadow edges and borders. Plants need to live cheek by jowl, so there is no room for bullies or show-offs. What you are trying to

Above – Live and let live. Daintiness and twinkling colour here soften the edge between hedge and grass.

Opposite above – By planting a circular area around the tree, the lawn becomes a path through a meadow leading to a seat. The plants at the foot of the tree echo those in the border.

Opposite below – The multiplicity of common names for Leucanthemum vulgare *–dog daisy, moon daisy, ox-eye daisy – reflect its ubiquity.*

design is a community that looks as though it has always been there and arose and developed of its own volition.

Where there are borders and paths, encourage plants to soften them by spilling over. After all, the very essence of a meadow is that it is relaxed and flows into its surroundings with no boundaries or sharp, straight lines. If you have a lawn, consider allowing a part of it to become a meadow by introducing perennials and biennials that will look after themselves. Use your mower to designate what is lawn and what is border. Choose areas where your little meadow looks most natural – around a tree, at the edge of shrubs, or in an out-of-the-way corner.

The tiniest meadow we ever made was for a garden at RHS Chelsea Flower Show, where in addition to a tiny piece of meadow alongside part of a perimeter native hedge, we planted up wide terracotta pots brimming with dainty grasses and flowers. They were buzzing with insects throughout the show and when we got them home our local bees and butterflies continued to enjoy them.

Vernal glories

In meadows and fields, both in the British Isles and in many other temperate regions, for a few celebratory weeks of the year, bulbs hold sway. Their performance transforms the grassy places they frequent, and though it is often short, it is spectacular. In the Pacific Northwest, quamash (*Camassia quamash*) paints meadows vivid blue, while in the mountains of southeastern Spain, Portugal, and southern France narcissi spread a bright yellow sheen over the grassy fields.

There are many good examples of bulb meadows in gardens where this idea is put into practice – sometimes embellished, sometimes as it would be in the wild. Christopher Lloyd was a keen and expert exponent of this practice at Great Dixter in Sussex, UK. Several of the RHS gardens boast bulb meadows, including RHS Rosemoor, which is my "local". Richard Lee, who gardened there during the period when the RHS took over the garden, grew literally thousands of *Narcissus cyclamineus* and *N. bulbocodium* from seed

*Above – Snake's head fritillary (*Fritillaria meleagris*) flourishes unfettered. The plain white or heavily tessellated flowers last only a few weeks. They are followed by seedheads that eventually burst, revealing stacks of paper-thin seedcases. On a dry, windy day, seed is blown hither and thither, increasing numbers and intensifying the effect.*

Above – Narcissus bulbocodium
is one of the best subjects for a bulb
meadow. Its behaviour is exemplary,
flowering in spring at only a few
centimetres high but with its dainty,
hoop-petticoat flowers well above
the grass. You can let it self-seed or, if
you are feeling enterprising, sow the
seeds thinly in seed trays. You will
need patience but it is well worth it.
A few specialist nurseries sell growing
plants; bulb merchants do not stock
it as dry bulbs.

for the new bulb meadows. Now the bulbs he grew so lovingly have increased and naturalized and give pleasure to thousands.

The closer a bulb is to the species, the better. There is always a simplicity and elegance to the results of nature's evolution. Too frequently plantings are rigid and the varieties chosen are big, brash and out of keeping for a bulb meadow. Ideally, bulbs should be given the opportunity to set and distribute seed before having their heads chopped off, so choose a part of the lawn where you are happy to leave well enough alone until seed has been dispersed. If a path in the lawn is designated and always mown, then the residue could become a bulb meadow. Necessarily, the grass will grow longer in the unmown areas, and if you encourage wild flowers and special grasses to take up residence within the meadow area, there will be colour and diversity throughout spring and summer. When eventually you cut the meadow in early autumn, shake the seed all over the area but rake up all the mowings. Never leave them, as it will enrich the soil – your meadow plants and bulbs need no extra nourishment.

Exotic scenes

Exotics? In a chapter about meadows? Surely not. At first glance, the two seem contradictory. Exotic means not native, though it is used in gardening circles to denote any tropical or subtropical plant.

But if you have a yen for Indian shot plant (*Canna*), dahlias, ginger lilies (*Hedychium*), and castor oil plant (*Ricinus*) with leaves like paddles or big hands, and at the same time love the informality of meadow planting, the two can be combined successfully without either being compromised. In our "hot" beds there is a backbone of shrubs, including a sinuous spine of box (*Buxus*) that runs through the two adjacent beds. There are perennials galore: coneflowers (*Rudbeckia*), heleniums, and spurge (*Euphorbia*), as well as clumps of crocosmia in glowing oranges, reds, and yellows; and in summer they are joined by a host of "exotic" subjects.

It is the way this community grows together that gives the planting a meadow feel and, despite so much of it being stage-managed, the effect is spontaneous and fits in with the rest of the garden – bananas (*Musa*) and all!

Opposite – Ginger lilies hail from Asia, from the foothills of the Himalayas. They have a reputation for being tender but some of them survive outdoors with protection. Their fascinating flowers arranged in spikes vary from white through yellow to orange (this magnificent variety is Hedychium *'Tara', bred by Tony Schilling and named after his daughter). All have wonderful paraphernalia, often in red, aimed at attracting insects. The majority are night scented.*

Below – At Glebe Cottage, our meadow – but a very exotic one – has bananas, castor oil plant, and gladioli, which bring extra verve to the usual subject.

Above left, centre, and right –
For me, a hugely important part
of maintaining my meadow planting
is this ethos of constant renewal and
reinvigoration by growing new plants
from home-collected seed (above left),
by deadheading (above centre), and
by dividing and replanting what is
there – when it needs it. As you keep
a watchful eye on how your planting
is developing, you become part of
your meadow.

Opposite – Pimpinella major *'Rosea'*
is a typically care-free meadow plant.

Meadow care

Meadow plantings are easy to maintain because tending your plot
is straightforward and a pleasure, whether you have a fully-fledged
true meadow with grasses, wild flowers, and, perhaps, bulbs, or
one planted in a looser way with cultivated perennials and grasses,
growing together in an informal but deliberately planned manner.

Even though the meadow planting style many of us subscribe to is
essentially that of a traditional herbaceous border – being composed
of herbaceous perennials and grasses – the ethos, the aesthetic, and
the upkeep are very different. For example, the welfare of wildlife
is intrinsic to the integrity of the meadow, and plants are chosen for
their informal feel and their ability to create a convivial community.
It is the involvement that you feel with a meadow planting that
separates it from the care of a traditional herbaceous border.

In modern meadows, plants are encouraged to be themselves.
Although deadheading, staking, and tidying up a bit are sometimes
appropriate, plants are generally left to their own devices.
Seedheads and dried stems are important elements of a meadow
planting during winter and are often left until spring, to be cleared
in time for the new growth of perennials and grasses.

A meadow planting aims to create a dynamic space with infinite
possibilities. Nothing stands still; it is constantly reinventing itself, and
changes from season to season. It involves us; we are in the planting,
experiencing it rather than standing on the outside as onlookers.

Fields Farm
- - - - - - - - - -

Deep in rural Shropshire, UK, the garden
of Fields Farm immerses you in the dynamic
planting around the house. The scale is
uncompromising, the style naturalistic and
welcoming – you want to explore and find
out what lies around the corner.
- -

Case study 12
- - - - - - - - - - - - - - - - - - - -

A Modern Meadow with a Personal Vision

*Above – When approaching a Victorian
red-brick house, you would expect neat
lawns and kempt borders, but not here
– instead, you are greeted by a melee
of statuesque plants and grasses.*

*Opposite – The garden at Fields Farm
is a dynamic place full of movement
and changing light. It nurtures the
classic plants that we have come
to associate with modern meadow
gardens – sedums, sages (Salvia),
and grasses – yet there are no clichés.
The planting is fresh, extrovert, and
unselfconscious. Glistening giant
feather grass (Stipa gigantea),
towards the end of its season, moves in
the breeze, in contrast to solid clumps
of Sedum 'Matrona'.*

THE GARDEN AT FIELDS FARM in the heart
of rural Shropshire, UK, is exciting, experimental, and innovative
– three words that its owner and chief gardener and designer,
Kirsty Grocott, has probably never used to describe it. It is her home
garden, 0.4ha (1 acre) of flat ground around her family house.

Many of the meadow plantings in the public eye are showcases
for nurseries or demonstrations of modern thinking about planting.
Despite their original image as being relaxed and easy-going spaces,
their exponents often have stringent formulae that qualify a scheme
either as a "meadow planting" or as a "prairie planting".

The cast of plants you encounter in such designs become familiar,
almost predictable – rather like the phenomenon of seeing the same
actors in different television dramas, even on a range of channels.
And very good some of them are too!

What is so refreshing about the garden at Fields Farm is that
an individual has embraced the whole ethos of meadow planting
and has impressed her own personality on it, her own take. For the
visitor, it is refreshing and invigorating. It is not just a question
of visiting and viewing; this garden is also involving – you are not
a spectator but a participant. Fields Farm is a place you are in and
experiencing; it is not something you view from the sidelines.

Above – Species plants or first-generation hybrids, as close as can be to their wild parents, are Kirsty's stock in trade. Here, Verbena bonariensis *is visited by the obligatory butterfly – it is hard to find verbena without such a winged creature.*

*Opposite above – Miss Willmott's ghost (*Eryngium giganteum*) makes itself at home anywhere and always looks the part in a meadow.*

*Opposite below – One of the classic prairie or meadow plants is coneflower (*Echinacea purpurea*).*

There is a broad track that runs around the garden, encouraging you to view it from various perspectives. Along the route, the same groupings of plants can be seen in different relationships: at one time, giant feather grass (*Stipa gigantea*) forms a wafty backdrop, mingling at its periphery with perovskia creating a lower storey, the pair making a backdrop for solid clumps of sedums; while from another perspective, the giant feather grass is the star of the show and you are encouraged to appreciate it in its own spectacular right, to take in its magnificent architecture.

The planting is not "in your face". It does not confront you but rather draws you in. There are recesses leading your eye into other plants, other parts of the garden. The same kind of feeling of freedom that Kirsty has created can be emulated in a much smaller space. People often provide a place for children to play, to kick a ball around, yet years afterwards, when the children of the house have become young people who seldom, if ever, visit the garden, the same layout persists. It has become entrenched. It is a manifestation of the same unwillingness to experiment that is displayed in so many

Above – Minnie rides her bike through what must feel like a giant's enchanted plot. Drying seedheads and tall airy grasses paint the picture; earlier, this would have been a greener picture, but for months now it has been full speed ahead, with summer perennials reaching their peak.

rooms, with furniture pushed up against the walls. I remember my grandad's back garden, some of it very formal with regimented beds and strips of lawn, but the bit to which we children always gravitated was the far patch with gigantic rhubarb (*Rheum*), mad, tall perennial sunflowers (*Helianthus*), and *Rosa* 'Dorothy Perkins', which rambled willy-nilly. This was our jungle, an incentive to invent our own games and use our imaginations. We had no meadows to ramble around in but how we looked forward to being involved in the anarchy of that piece of ground.

Though many of the plants at Fields Farm have been seen before in the context of meadow gardening, the visitor gets a whole new take on them here. There is nothing trite or formulaic. You feel as though Kirsty has consulted the place and it has decided where plants need to be. Many of the plants she has chosen are accommodating and straightforward. They need little in the way of maintenance. She does not stake and, apart from deadheading and cutting back when there are no seedheads required, the garden is not demanding. The plants are suitable for the soil and situation –

*Above – It is the spaces and the surfaces in the garden that set the scene for magnificent bursts of flowers or seedheads. A circular bed cobbled with beach pebbles separates the garden from the track (drive) and also enhances the clumps of sea hollies (*Eryngium*).*

*Overleaf – Almost the entire family of Apiaceae offers plateaux of tiny flowers, followed by attractive seedheads that often make just as much of a contribution to the garden aesthetic. Such heads are rigid and architectural and combine dramatically with more mobile plants, as here with giant feather grass (*Stipa gigantea*).*

in any successful garden (by which I mean any garden where plants are thriving and happy), priorities must always be that way round.

Most meadow gardens are at their best between high summer and late autumn. In fact, many of the plants from the American prairies that feature large in such gardens reach their peak in early and mid-autumn. The scenes here would have been very different in the summer months, being greener, more tussocky. Later, the all-consuming mellowness that overtakes all meadowy gardens changes the colours to russet and gold.

All the pictures here of Kirsty's garden capture it on a particular day, but, like all our gardens, it changes during each day according to the weather, and from day to day, week to week, season to season.

One of the most wonderful factors about such meadow gardens composed of perennials and grasses is this "life-in-time" that they possess. It is like glorying in a thousand different gardens. For me, this is their great attraction. They have a life of their own, and if you make such a garden, you have no option other than to go along with it – or at least to cooperate with it.

The Garden House

At one time, The Garden House, near Dartmoor, UK, under the auspices of Lionel Fortescue, had a much more traditional style. It has, however, moved with the times and, thanks in great part to Keith Wiley's intervention, parts of it exude a wonderful, whimsical quality that joins the garden to the landscape beyond.

Case study 13

Following Nature's Cue

Above – You hardly notice you are walking on a path, so entranced do you become by the rich mixture of wild flowers and their closely related cultivated cousins that compose this delightful meadow planting.

Opposite – Here, there is no path at all – the meadow is in total and joyous control. Close by, the Norman church of Buckland Monachorum and, in the distance, the view of Dartmoor add a timeless quality to the scene.

ALTHOUGH THE GARDEN HOUSE is steeped in tradition – be it mainly from the twentieth century – it is also famed as a place of experimentation and excellent practice, especially in its meadow plantings.

I have to declare an interest in including The Garden House as one of my three meadow gardens. It has long been a personal favourite. Each time I walk through its gates, I feel the same rush of excitement that I experienced the first time I visited and, after being there an hour or so, a similar sense of tranquillity. It is a garden that puts you at your ease.

There is much to look at: rhododendrons and collections of rare shrubs and trees with the best provenance (Lionel Fortescue, who started the garden, was an authority); a sunken garden with a tower to view it from above; and the renowned herbaceous borders with their meadowy appeal. If it is summer, the meadow areas are the first port of call. Some of the schemes have been specifically planned and executed as meadow plantings; they have had, and still have, enormous influence among proponents of this discipline.

For 25 years, Keith Wiley, now renowned for his Wildside garden (see p.128) just up the road, gave his heart and soul to The Garden House. He was constantly innovating, coming up not only with new

*Left, above, and overleaf – One of the archetypal meadow plants, meadow cranesbill (*Geranium pratense*) is a British native that you may now glimpse on road verges and field edges but it would once have been a denizen of the meadow. It fits all the criteria sought in a meadow plant: it is robust yet poetic and mixes happily with visitors such as* Knautia macedonica *(left) and other indigenous plants, grasses, buttercups (*Ranunculus*), and campions (*Silene*) (above and overleaf).*

ideas but also new takes on the traditional. Keith is hugely observant of, and sensitive to, the wild landscape – wherever that may be. After visiting the veld in its glory during a South African spring, he was inspired to adopt the idea at The Garden House.

I have heard people criticize the planting of the subsequent meadow, saying it is not pure, and that some of the species within it are not South African. Such comments miss the point. What Keith wanted to design was not a carbon copy of what he had seen. He wished to capture the spirit of the place, its energy, and vigour. He knew that a literal transfer of all the species that he saw flowering on the veld to a chunk of land on the edge of Dartmoor would have been unsuccessful. Instead, he searched out and brought together flowers and grasses that would produce the same effect, regardless of their origins and provenance. Thus the meadows at The Garden House are about interpreting a reality and enabling it to work in the same way in a very different location and using different plants.

Above left – Columbines lend themselves to meadow mixes, gently self-seeding and rubbing shoulders with the aristocracy or the hoi polloi – in this case, campions.

Above right – If this were a corn meadow, you would expect to see red-flowered corn poppies (Papaver rhoeas), *but, instead, the papery petals of a pink Icelandic poppy* (P. nudicaule) *merge into the picture perfectly.*

There are several areas of meadow at The Garden House. In some places they comprise mainly native wild flowers, while in other places these are joined by familiar plants from similar locations in temperate regions all over the world, particularly in the northern hemisphere. In the native meadows are to be found buttercups (*Ranunculus*), campions (*Silene*), and cranesbills (*Geranium*), joined by dog daisies (*Leucanthemum vulgare*). In the other meadow type, columbine (*Aquilegia*), knautia, meadow rue (*Thalictrum*), poppies (*Papaver*), and umbelliferous plants swell the guest list.

Keith is past master at creating beautiful meadows but they are an idea that anyone can emulate given a piece of sunny, reasonably well-drained ground and the inspiration from nature.

If you are starting a meadow for the first time, ensure that the site is suitable. It should preferably be in full sun for most of the day. Shade and meadows do not mix, as overhanging trees will make these plants sparse and etiolated.

Above left and right – There is room for many flower shapes in a meadow planting, from the neat spikes of catmint (Nepeta) *(above left), with their myriad tiny flowers, which are a rich source of nectar for pollinating insects, to the small clusters of flowers on a tall spike on Jacob's ladder* (Polemonium, *above right), which open in succession. The latter self-seeds readily, which is an attractive characteristic for gardeners and insects alike.*

Reams have been written about wild flowers thriving best on poor soils, but to change soil radically is a pretty massive proposition. If your soil is very fertile, then it may be worth taking some of it away. You can add grit or gravel to impoverish the soil, but is it not far better to grow species that thrive in the existing conditions?

Plant choice and combinations are the keys to helping your meadow flourish. Looking to your locality to see what does well is the first clue. It is easier to do this detective work if you live deep in the country but still plausible in the middle of the city. Parks, other people's gardens, and waste ground can all offer information and guidance. If you are gardening on heavy clay, a perennial meadow with buttercups and a mix of suitable grasses as its mainstay could be a good choice for your meadow.

Having cleared the ground of perennial weeds, you can sow directly into a well-prepared seedbed or else into seed trays. Seed can be sown in autumn or spring, but if your soil is very wet and heavy, spring is usually preferable.

271

Marchants

As you walk into the garden at Marchants in East Sussex, UK, you are overtaken by the desire to explore as one wonderful planting association takes over from another, each original and often adventurous. Even then the whole is greater than the sum of the parts, and the garden is cohesive, woven from a rich mix of plants and ideas.

Case study 14

The Meadow Moves Gently into Autumn

Above – Curved areas of the meadow provide boundaries for the ebullient planting.

Opposite – Seedheads of African blue lily (Agapanthus), phlomis, coneflower (Rudbeckia), and heleniums, all in generous clumps alongside the fresh, pink accents of an annual – kiss-me-quick-over-the-garden-gate (Persicaria orientalis) – here make a beautifully rounded and satisfying picture. The flowers that preceded the seedheads would have been truly spectacular.

VERY FEW GARDENS MAKE you smile continuously. The only reason you stop smiling at Marchants is because you are momentarily concentrating on some glorious combination of plants, or some innovative idea, and then, when you have taken it in and appreciated it, you start smiling again.

Here is a garden that offers a completely personal take on meadow planting. It displays a wonderful combination of plants for their own sake and for their skilful juxtapositions. For this is what Marchants's creator, Graham Gough, is – a plantsman and an aesthete.

Graham loves plants. He relishes them for themselves and he adores them as the material with which to fashion meadow pictures that move through space and time. For a long time he worked with Elizabeth Strangman, whose Washfield nursery for the last 30 years of the twentieth century was at the forefront of introducing, propagating, and bringing to the gardening public's attention the very best perennials and grasses. Many of the plants Graham now uses at Marchants have their antecedents at Washfield or, in some cases, are the same varieties as those that were grown there.

But it is not just what he grows but how he has put his plants together that makes this garden. Here, Graham designs with plants.

273

Above – Mounds of flowers and foliage spill over the path, creating a three-dimensional picture, so that the path – a means to take us on a wonderful tour of discovery – is forgotten.

Opposite above left, above right, below left, and below right – Depth in the planting has been achieved by intermingling grasses and perennial plants: Gaura lindheimeri *(above left);* miscanthus, molinia, and coneflower (Rudbeckia) *(above right);* Verbena and eragrostis *(below left); and* Malva cannabinum *(below right).*

He makes marriages and they are almost always happy. There are bold contrasts and subtle harmonies.

The Marchants meadow beds are rich and varied; they are full of surprises too. Graham uses annuals imaginatively, providing gentle movement and emphasis to link one part of the bed to another. Sometimes they are not so subtle. There may be a sprinkling of attention-grabbing orange, vivid yellow, or red provided by California poppies (*Eschscholzia*) or fiery cosmos that concentrates your eye in one particular area or encourages you to go on to more laid-back subjects. Such is the nature of meadows that there is an underrunning pattern, as well as highlights of intense colour. However, it is not exclusively colour that Graham thinks about in his designs. Form, pattern, and texture are equally important factors, as well as how the layout of the garden relates to the landscape beyond.

There is no invitation here to step into the beds, to walk through the planting, yet at all times you feel you are strolling through a meadow. The beds are designed in such a way that you can access all the planting from every side so you truly feel you are in among it.

Above – As autumn descends, plants present a more abstract picture with structural seedheads in their prime.

Opposite – Heads of globe artichoke (Cynara scolymus) *look beautiful while in their death throes.*

Previous page above – Prairie plants and others mix and mingle as the autumn begins to assert itself and reach the height of its spectacular annual performance at Marchants.

Previous page below – A few weeks later on into autumn, the grasses and seedheads now predominate in the same area.

Marchants is a sizeable garden, yet its planting and the aesthetic that informs it are very pertinent to many a smaller garden where the gardener aspires to a meadowy feel, a modern style, and a space full of beautiful plants. One of the advantages that a meadow planting with perennials and grasses such as this has over a summer-flowering meadow, which is strictly managed and cut back hard in early autumn, is that here is a space that is enjoyed throughout the year. The wealth of texture, colour, and form at Marchants continues from early summer through to late winter (there are other attractions in between but they probably do not meet the meadow brief). Thus Marchants could be a blueprint for many a smaller space in a city, suburban, or country garden.

One of the glories of the stalwart perennials and exciting grasses that form the backbone of the garden at Marchants is that they provide a revolving calendar, a picture that celebrates each season in the garden and in Nature more broadly. Making the most of every month in the garden is especially important when space is at a premium. This sort of meadow planting is within the reaches of most people.

Meadow plant directory

***Centaurea montana* cultivar**
No plant could be more simple and straightforward to grow than perennial cornflower (*Centaurea montana*), as well as give such rich rewards. It is a real cottage-garden favourite that looks wonderful when mixed with other plants in any modern meadow setting. It is usually seen in blue but pictured here is a lavender-coloured cultivar.

Gaura lindheimeri
This has to be one of the prettiest plants around. It looks as if a whole flock of butterflies has decided to settle on its twiggy branches. Being light, airy, and the perfect mixer, it never crowds out other plants, but always looks at ease. Although it is not long-lived, once you have grown it, you will find it indispensable. Take little cuttings in spring.

Trifolium ochroleucon
A clover and a half! This splendid bush, up to 50cm (20in) tall, with its soft colouring, goes with just about everything, but particularly pastels. Clover (*Trifolium ochroleucon*) flowers from early summer for at least two months, and this can be encouraged by cutting individual heads back to an emerging flower bud; propagate from basal cuttings.

Geranium pratense
Meadow cranesbill (*Geranium pratense*) is one of the most desirable of plants. It looks lovely in the wild mingling with grasses. British writer and naturalist Geoffrey Grigson said it looked like an encampment of gypsies. I love it in the garden even though it has only one flowering, from early to mid-summer. If you let it seed you will get great billowing clouds of it.

***Aster* 'Little Carlow'**
This has to be my favourite Michaelmas daisy (*Aster*). It is a form of the wood aster, so it will tolerate some shade. *Aster* 'Little Carlow' produces tall stems full of myriad, tiny, blue daisies. It is incredibly attractive to butterflies, and it flowers just at the time when the autumn hatch of butterflies is on the wing.

Echinacea purpurea

At one time the only coneflowers (*Echinacea*) you could buy were pink or white but recently there has been an influx of yellow, apricot – all sorts of gorgeous shades. Sadly, they do not like my heavy clay, preferring a loamy, lighter, even quite sandy soil. They are absolutely brilliant, especially when mixed with grasses and yarrow (*Achillea*).

Eupatorium purpureum

Joe Pye weed (*Eupatorium purpureum*) is an American plant that is extremely popular with modern garden designers in a meadowy setting. It is great for butterflies, as it does not flower until autumn, when nectar and pollen are in high demand. Its heads of small, fluffy, pink flowers do not last long, so deadhead to prolong the display.

Phlox maculata

All phlox make good border plants and are brilliant in any kind of meadow mix. With their long corolla tube, they provide invaluable pollen and nectar for moths and other night-flying insects. Phlox come in a wide range of colours, but the ones that look most lovely in the evening are those with white, pale lavender-blue, and soft pink flowers.

Echinops ritro 'Veitch's Blue'

Most of us are familiar with globe thistle (*Echinops ritro*). It is often a rather wishy-washy colour, but in *E. r.* 'Veitch's Blue' the colour is very definite. These deep blue globes atop white stems with lovely, silvery grey foliage make a striking feature in any border. They are also really good neighbours and mix well with other plants.

Astrantia 'Roma'

This is a sterile form of Hattie's pincushion (*Astrantia*), so no seed is produced. The benefit to the gardener is that it keeps on flowering for ages, provided it is deadheaded – something we do not do with other astrantias. As *A.* 'Roma' also bears a second flush of flowers, these glorious, pink pincushions continue right the way into mid-autumn.

Sedum 'Herbstfreude'

This is one of the best sedum and among the most prolific, with its huge, almost cauliflower-like flower heads. The flowers can be retained after blooming so they develop their invaluable seed, which birds love. The biggest attraction of sedum for wildlife, particularly butterflies, is the flowers. It is often called the butterfly plant.

Salvia nemorosa

These herbaceous sages (*Salvia*) provide a splendid, vertical axis in a meadow planting, which usually comprises lots of soft-mounding plants. They come in a range of colours, mainly blues, purples, and pinks, and even when the flowers have fallen, the bracts remain and are extremely attractive. They are also brilliant insect plants.

Cirsium rivulare 'Atropurpureum'

Thistles (*Cirsium*) have become extremely fashionable in recent years and in most cases with very good reason. This is one of my favourites. It looks as though somebody has taken their scissors to these rich crimson flowers and trimmed them neatly. The leaves are marvellous at first but shabby later on, so once it has flowered, chop it down to the ground.

Papaver orientale 'Patty's Plum'

Oriental poppies (*Papaver orientale*) are like shooting stars. They last only a few days but once they are there, there is nothing like them. After flowering they can be sheared to the ground, and with a bit of luck they will flower again. But even if they bloom just once, nothing surpasses them for sheer theatrical effect, particularly *P. o.* 'Patty's Plum'.

Campanula lactiflora 'Prichard's Variety'

Though milky bellflower (*Campanula lactiflora*) usually flowers in shades of white and pale blue, *C. l.* 'Prichard's Variety' has very deep blue blooms. Stems, sometimes to 2m (6½ft) tall, bear heads of tiny bellflowers. Once the first truss has opened, the flowering stem can be cut back so further flowers develop on laterals.

Vernonia fasciculata

This American plant flowers from mid-summer through to early or mid-autumn and it looks great with yellow autumn daisies, such as sunflowers (*Helianthus*) and coneflowers (*Rudbeckia*). Ironweed (*Vernonia fasciculata*) can grow up to 2m (6½ft) high, but if you want it to be shorter, cut down its growth to within 30cm (1ft) of the ground in early summer.

Hemerocallis 'Stafford'

There are more varieties of daylilies (*Hemerocallis*) than there are of almost any other flowering plant. They have been hybridized furiously and are incredibly popular in the US and northern European gardens. The range of colours is immense and most of them look brilliant with other plants. I love *H.* 'Stafford' alongside bronze fennel (*Foeniculum*).

Crocosmia

These have had a renaissance during the last few years, as people have realized what useful plants they are and what beauties too. Dig up the corms every couple of years, take the top corm off, and discard the rest. Replant in some good, fertile soil. There are plenty of different varieties in various shades of yellow and orange to choose from.

Phlomis fruticosa

Jerusalem sage (*Phlomis fruticosa*) is a striking shrub with silvery grey foliage and mustard-coloured flowers in whorls up and down the stems. The whole plant is covered with soft, woolly hairs and is very soft to the touch. The hairs protect the cuticle of the leaf and that of the stem against hot sun. It has a very wide root run.

Helianthus 'Lemon Queen'

The perennial sunflowers (*Helianthus*) provide a real dash of panache in the late border. I am especially fond of this one with its pale lemon-yellow colouring. There is nothing brash about it. It is a thug in some ways, though, because it spreads furiously and you really have to keep on top of it, but I would never be without it.

Achillea filipendulina 'Cloth of Gold'

In traditional borders and modern plantings, yarrows (*Achillea*) look perfectly at home. At one time, *A. filipendulina* 'Cloth of Gold' was typical of yarrows grown – nearly all had stout, stiff stems and flat heads and lots of tiny, bright yellow flowers. Nowadays there are numerous different-coloured hybrids.

Rudbeckia fulgida var. deamii

All summer long, black-eyed Susan (*Rudbeckia fulgida*) is a quiet, green presence but from early autumn – even right through to late autumn – the yellow daisies burst forth with their conical, black centres. My brick garden here is full of this plant and it just makes the autumn. It spreads easily and will even cope with heavy clay. It is an ideal meadow mixer.

Molinia

Of all the grasses now used in meadow plantings, molinias have to be my favourites. They are so versatile. Early in summer their inflorescences are purple and blue but in autumn the whole plant changes to splendid, sparkling gold. They persist until a severe frost comes, after which the whole plant collapses on the ground, making it easy to tidy up.

Author acknowledgements

I owe so much thanks to so many people for helping me to write this book, especially my family, Neil, Annie, and Alice. Thanks to Alison Starling, my publisher, for her continuing enthusiasm and excitement for the project and her determination and patience in bringing it all to fruition. Thanks also to her behind-the-scenes team who have turned my dream into a reality, and especially to Joanna Chisholm, our copy editor, for banging it all into shape. Thanks to Gordon Wise, my literary agent, for all his efforts to arrange this project and make it run smoothly. Special thanks to my friend Janine Wookey for understanding what I was looking for in our case studies before I knew it myself. She worked tirelessly to find the best locations. Ginny Hearn gave me good-humoured and invaluable assistance in typing up the plant directories. As ever, it has been a delight to work with Jonathan Buckley, whose exquisite photographs really make the book and inspire me to try to match them with my words. This time there were two Jonathans! It has been a pleasure to work with Creative Director Jonathan Christie, whose design for our book is outstanding. A huge thank you to the gardeners who have created the gardens that feature as our Case Studies. They are an inspiration to anyone trying to make a beautiful garden in harmony with nature.

Garden credits

The author, photographer, and publisher would like to thank the following people for all their help making this book possible.

p.14 Sue and Wol Staines, Glen Chantry, Essex; p.16 John Massey, Ashwood Nurseries, West Midlands; p.18 The National Trust, Dunham Massey, Cheshire; pp.20–1 The National Trust, Sissinghurst Castle, Kent; p.22 John Massey, Ashwood Nurseries, West Midlands; p.27 Nigel Dunnett, RBC Blue Water Garden, RHS Chelsea Flower Show 2012; p.28 Helen Yemm, Eldenhurst, East Sussex; p.29 The National Trust, Hidcote, Gloucestershire; p.64 Sue and Wol Staines, Glen Chantry, Essex; p.66 St Michael's Mount, Cornwall; p.69 Liz Shackleton, West Sussex; pp.70–1 St Michael's Mount, Cornwall; p.75 tl Stephen Firth, RHS Chelsea Flower Show; p.75 tr Virginia Kennedy, London; p.75 bl Liz Shackleton, West Sussex; p.75 br Wendy and Leslie Howell, The Watch, Sussex; p.76 St Michael's Mount, Cornwall; p.113 Tom Stuart-Smith, Broughton Grange, Oxfordshire; p.116 St Michael's Mount, Cornwall; pp.118–19 John Massey, Ashwood Nurseries, West Midlands; p.122 and p.123 Kevin Hughes; p.124 Julian and Isabel Bannerman, Hanham Court, South Gloucestershire; p.125 br David and Mavis Seeney, Upper Mill Cottage, Kent; p.127 Carol Misch, Cornwall; p.154 The National Trust, Sissinghurst Castle, Kent; pp.158–9 The Garden House, Devon; p.163 Graham Gough, Marchants, East Sussex; p.192 The National Trust, Hidcote, Gloucestershire; p.196 The Garden House, Devon; p.197 l Sue and Wol Staines, Glen Chantry, Essex; p.197 r Chatsworth House, Derbyshire; pp.198–9 Keith Wiley, Wildside, Devon; p.200 Marwood Hill Gardens, North Devon; p.202 Helen Yemm, Eldenhurst, East Sussex; p.203 Dr and Mrs Robert Moule, Chygurno Cornwall; p.205 Sue and Wol Staines, Glen Chantry, Essex; p.206 John Massey, Ashwood Nurseries, West Midlands; p.207 Keith Wiley, Wildside, Devon; p.208 Christopher Lloyd, Great Dixter, East Sussex; p.209 Alan Titchmarsh, Hampshire; p.244 and p.245 Keith Wiley, Wildside, Devon; p.248 and p.249 Helen Yemm, Eldenhurst, East Sussex; p.250 and p.251 Christopher Lloyd, Great Dixter, East Sussex.

Publisher: Alison Starling
Creative Director: Jonathan Christie
Senior Editor: Leanne Bryan
Copy Editor: Joanna Chisholm
Proofreader: Helen Ridge
Indexer: Helen Snaith
Assistant Production Manager: Caroline Alberti
Location Consultant: Janine Wookey

An Hachette UK Company
www.hachette.co.uk

First published in Great Britain in 2015 by Mitchell Beazley, a division of Octopus Publishing Group Ltd, Carmelite House, 50 Victoria Embankment, London EC4Y 0DZ
www.octopusbooks.co.uk
www.octopusbooksusa.com

Design and layout copyright © Octopus Publishing Group Ltd 2015

Text copyright © Carol Klein 2015

Photography copyright © Jonathan Buckley 2015

Distributed in the US by Hachette Book Group, 1290 Avenue of the Americas, 4th and 5th Floors, New York, NY 10020

Distributed in Canada by Canadian Manda Group, 664 Annette St., Toronto, Ontario, Canada M6S 2C8

UK ISBN: 978-1-84533-797-1
US/Can ISBN: 978-1-84533-956-2

A CIP record for this book is available from the British Library.

Printed and bound in China.

10 9 8 7 6 5 4 3 2 1

Carol Klein is a much-loved author, television presenter, and passionate plantswoman. Carol has been a regular presenter on the BBC's flagship gardening programme, *BBC Gardeners' World*, for more than a decade. Her nursery, Glebe Cottage Plants, won six gold medals at the RHS Chelsea Flower Show. Her bestselling books include *RHS Grow Your Own Veg*, *RHS Grow Your Own Fruit*, *Carol Klein's Favourite Plants*, *Grow Your Own Garden*, and *Life in a Cottage Garden*. She's a regular contributor to *BBC Gardeners' World* magazine and *Gardens Illustrated*, and writes weekly columns for the *Sunday Mirror* and *Garden News*. Carol's Devon garden, Glebe Cottage, where she has lived for 35 years, has become world famous for its glorious planting inspired by the rules of nature.

Jonathan Buckley is a specialist garden and flower photographer who has worked closely with Carol Klein for many years, photographing her garden at Glebe Cottage. He has also collaborated with Christopher Lloyd, Sarah Raven, and Alan Titchmarsh. His book projects include Sarah Raven's *Wild Flowers*, Alan Titchmarsh's *My Secret Garden*, and Carol Klein's *Life in a Cottage Garden*. The Garden Media Guild has awarded him Photographer of the Year, Features Photographer of the Year, and Single Image of the Year.